welcome to your

Facelift

welcome to your

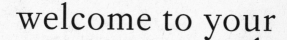

Facelift

what to expect before, during, and after cosmetic surgery

HELEN BRANSFORD

MAIN
STREET
BOOKS

Doubleday New York London Toronto Sydney Auckland

A MAIN STREET BOOK
PUBLISHED BY DOUBLEDAY
a division of Bantam Doubleday Dell Publishing Group, Inc.
1540 Broadway, New York, New York 10036

MAIN STREET BOOKS, DOUBLEDAY, and the portrayal of a building with a tree are
trademarks of Doubleday, a division of Bantam Doubleday Dell
Publishing Group, Inc.

The Library of Congress has cataloged the Doubleday hardcover edition
of this book as follows:

Bransford, Helen.
Welcome to your facelift: what to expect before, during, and
after cosmetic surgery / Helen Bransford. — 1st ed.
p. cm.
1. Facelift—Popular works. I. Title.
RD119.5.F33B73 1997
617.5'20592—dc21 96-51774
CIP

ISBN 0-385-48550-6

First Main Street Books Edition: January 1998

1 3 5 7 9 10 8 6 4 2

for

Bill Goldman

the best lift of all

and

my cherished guinea pig

Suzanne

Contents

Author's Notes

Any statistics I have quoted, unless otherwise stated, are courtesy of the American Society of Plastic and Reconstructive Surgeons, whose professional and thorough surveys are conducted in even-numbered years.

The doctors referred to throughout this book are listed alphabetically in the Appendix, along with the city in which they practice. The great majority of these I have interviewed directly; in the remaining cases, I have interviewed three or more of the doctor's patients.

Except in specific instances, and for the sake of expedience, I will be referring to all plastic surgeons as male and all patients as female. Though this may be politically heinous, current estimations are that by the year 2000 as many as 9 percent or 10 percent of plastic surgeons may be women.

I would like to specially thank Cathy Follin, Wendy Lewis, Nancy Kobus, and Dr. Eileen Redden, Ph.D.

Foreword

by Ivo Pitanguy, M.D.

At the end of the twentieth century, society races into the future at an ever-increasing rate. At the same time, individuals seem to be left behind, perplexed. Loneliness, social exclusion, and professional disappointments are problems that afflict people on an almost epidemic scale. Paradoxically, the search for happiness and well-being has never been so emphasized in all aspects of modern civilization: recreation, sports, technology. Global media create universal standards and values and dictate what people should eat, dress, and look like. Looking good has become an informal championship in which everyone participates and which everyone desires to win. Physical beauty is synonymous with success, and likewise unattractiveness spells defeat. People no longer passively accept natural deformities or the defects that the aging process imposes so unmercifully.

It appears natural, then, that plastic surgery has developed into a household expression. For those who must battle the consequences of physical imperfection, the plastic surgeon is the valuable knight at hand, and aesthetic surgical procedures the weapons with which to correct what Mother Nature has too generously bestowed or to fend off the constant assault of wrinkles, sagging skin, and fatty pouches.

Helen Bransford's manual on cosmetic facial surgery is a confident report from the battlefront. She recounts her experience as a patient while at the same time giving us an overview of the myriad procedures available for the correction of the aging face. Her personal thoughts are interspersed with many interviews with some of the most highly respected surgeons and dermatologists in the United States. This makes the book a pleasure to read, amusing without being shallow, addressing such disparate topics as the psychological motivations for surgery, planned procedures for different age groups and ethnic backgrounds, and what realistically to expect from a facelift. The patient who is considering a "new look," with all the ambiguity that this expression implies, will find the book both informative and educational.

—Rio de Janeiro, November 1996

Head Professor of the Post-Graduation and Master's Courses in Plastic Surgery of the Pontifical Catholic University of Rio de Janeiro and the Carlos Chagas Post-Graduate Medical Institute. Member of the Brazilian Society of Plastic Surgery, of the National Academy of Medicine, and the National Academy of Letters. F.I.C.S., F.A.C.S.

welcome to your

1
welcome to
your facelift

A pleasing countenance is no slight advantage.

—Ovid

i always knew there'd be a price to pay for marrying a man seven years younger than I am. I just wasn't sure what it would be. We had made it through almost four years of marriage feeling joined at the hip and soul, when, on a quiet summer night, I heard the first shoe drop and I forgot to remember to breathe. Not a boot, just a soft slipper, but its echo stayed in the room. He was interviewing Julia Roberts for a magazine profile and came home from their first dinner smitten. He shared with me thirty or forty of her virtues, her remarkable physical attributes, and her ability to quote lines from Hemingway stories. Then he said with astonishment, "She's almost as funny as you are." I asked if this intergalactic goddess had any idea he was married. "Oh sure," he said. "I told her all about you. Well, everything but your age. I didn't tell her that."

I desperately wanted to deny what I was hearing, but his words stung the air. He had wanted to protect me of course, from the world's knowing my age relative to his own. Only then did I understand that the age issue was harder for him than for me. I might add here that he frequently quotes himself with, "It's not whether you win or lose in life, it's how you look playing the game."

The next morning I started calling doctors.

Mama had never exploited her looks, but there's no question she was right up there with Garbo and Babe Paley. In London and every corner of America I ever visited, some dignified old geezer would lean over his cane misty-eyed and begin muttering about the most beautiful woman he'd ever known. Though compromised by age, a certain dapperness clung to these gents, and I could tell they knew their stuff. I was gracious and agreed with them (because they were right), quickly adding that I was the image of my father, so they wouldn't fear they had damaged my self-esteem. My mother was an arresting beauty with alabaster skin and 200-watt blue eyes. I am a virtual albino with dull red hair, the image of my father, who, though he was a firecracker, was already technically bald when we met in the maternity ward.

Blessedly, Mama played down her looks and stressed good values. Her arsenal of beauty products tended to be Nivea oil, Frownies, the rare lipstick, and a steadfast rejection of the sun. I have often compared photos of us at various stages of youth. Mama at sixteen, dressed entirely in fur on the deck of an Alaska-bound ship. Then me at sixteen, twin of Alfred E. Neuman, proudly hugging my rugged pet goat. I was indisputably born to sack groceries, while, like the Dalai Lama removed from his homeland, it was her destiny to be an empress wherever she lived.

Thank God she loved me. I don't remember a moment of doubt on that score. But the fact of her blind devotion presented a special problem for me: Her adoration sadly disqualified her completely from making rational comments about my looks. Even at my pale, snaggle-toothed, clumsy worst, she would swear I was sublime. Her irrational loyalty endeared her to me far beyond this life. But I knew at nine to take it for what it was, and look elsewhere for the truth, however cruel it might be.

Redheads are an acquired taste. We feel different and pale, our lashes and brows are invisible, and we know early on to concentrate on personality and humor. Unless we've applied eyeliner and a browstick, we simply don't show up in a room.

Mama's keen eye foresaw the problem well. When I was sixteen, she delivered me to the best makeup artists of the day in both Rome and New York (Eve of Roma and Eddie Senz respectively, in case anyone's been alive long enough to remember them). She explained to Mr. Senz that I needed help in learning to emphasize my eyes, and guidance in finding colors to match my hair. Then the maestro himself leaned into my face in an attempt to please my mother, saying, "The world will be your oyster, my dear," at which point I hit rock bottom. Yards of steel wire confounded my errant teeth as I slumped toward the mirror, flabby, gawky, freckled, and pale. I wept to be home brushing my pony, who adored me for the smell of apples and never once scrutinized my face. I dreaded my future as a girl, as only an albino can.

Though things improved with time, my self-image was die-struck that humiliating afternoon.

With shocking frequency, it is now repeated that until the age of twenty-one, the way you look depends on your parents and God. After twenty-one, it's all up to you—provided you have the cash or can qualify for credit.

A few easily attainable changes include body shape (addition of curves, removal of curves), freshening skin texture, removing wrinkles, deleting tummy fat, deleting *any* fat, remounting a droopy butt, lifting saggy eyelids, removing bulges beneath the eyes, supplementing thinning hair, and altering details of the facial profile (reshaping the nose, augmenting or reducing the chin for balance, implanting artificial cheekbones, and defatting the chin and throat). But as I am determined to focus here on facial possibilities alone, I will not be discussing the myriad configurations of work that can be done "below the neck." Nor will I cover breast augmentation or nose jobs, which are generally dealt with during one's teens or early twenties these days. In the likely event your life revolves around a budget, doing any of these procedures piecemeal works quite well. A nip here, a tuck there, two years later a peel and some minor lipo. Many doctors, in fact, advise patients to have a sequence of small procedures over the years rather than a sudden and more obvious overhaul.

> *There is a certain melancholy in seeing oneself rot.*
> —Katharine Hepburn

who can argue with photos?
(like, for example, twelve or more)

In fairness to my groom at the time of his life-changing comment I hadn't seen a recognizable snapshot of myself in several years. Each one contained the withered, leathery version of a thirty-five-year-old redhead I once knew well, and I fell into the habit of slipping them face-down into the nearest drawer. I was repeatedly puzzled that Sonia Rykiel could wander so frequently into photos of my family and friends. Then I would reach for my glasses and slowly bring into focus the fact that the Sonia character was me. While Ms. Rykiel is electrifyingly chic for seventy, I was crushed.

Along with a younger husband, I also have infant children. Rounding out the cliché Second Marriage—but with conventional genders reversed. I mention this because any day now a well-meaning caretaker will no doubt announce to a room of twentysomething mothers that "we have a special visitor, a grandmother braving the elements to pick up her charge." The mothers will turn with sappy smiles, and it will be me standing there behind them—wishing I had on huge arresting sunglasses with my spike-tip leopard print heels, and once again feeling an idiotic sadness that I can't blend in with the group.

how i got from there to here

If asked under hypnosis, I'd answer to feeling thirty-six or seven. Attitudinally at least, and maybe physically too. Sadly this estimate's off by a mile. Next, there's the visual aspect to consider. How old do I look to myself? I close my eyes and clutch, but no image floats into view. Instead, I remember my father telling me before he died in his late seventies that he had the mind and curiosity of a man in his twenties, but to his enormous aggravation, his body was wearing out (which leads me to suspect that none of us accurately perceives our own state of decrepitude.)

While my mind doesn't seem to be maturing much, my face has compensated by not missing a beat. The reverse could have been nice. This leaves me, I figure, with a nebulous self-image ranging loosely between four and ninety-four. My subconscious eye has utterly refused to log anything past thirty-five. How, then, did I wake up a decade later stumbling around in seared skin and sporting wrinkles like I've never seen on anybody? The answer probably coincides with my sudden inability to read print closer than two feet away. Impaired vision may be proof of God's empathy for the onset of middle age. Unfortunately, however, middle age is past the eleventh hour for anyone planning to enter the race toward serious cosmetic maintenance. So, what with Ms. Rykiel grinning back at me from photos, late-life parenthood, and Julia Roberts flashing through my marriage, I was ready for a radical leap. Lumped together in neon green, these phenomena comprised my Trigger Event, the springboard that nudged me well beyond the line of hesitation, gasping for an aesthetic airlift.

so what is a trigger event?

A Trigger Event can happen any time or any place to an adult of any age. It can be a comment from a stranger or a criticism overheard. It may be an awkward attempt at praise that fails and goes belly up. It can be an insult hurled in anger, or a passing glance in a well-lit mirror. It can even be seeing the positive results of a friend's cosmetic surgery. The Trigger Event forces us to suddenly reconsider our physical selves—and to assess ourselves objectively—as a new acquaintance might see us.

It can be straightforward and simple: One spouse dies and the survivor grieves. When it's time to consider dating again, the survivor is paralyzed with fear and needs a crutch to get back in the ring. She might have undressed and removed her makeup for only one person in the last thirty years.

Whatever it is, a Trigger Event has to occur naturally. Contrived, it would have no effect. A simple example is a woman's realization that she is presumed by others to be pregnant, when she is simply overweight. A stranger's comments along these lines can prompt a commitment to fitness that no amount of cajoling could have prompted before. Another potential Trigger Event is the hapless perception that a younger sister is the older. That the mother of a child is that child's grandmother. And worst of all, that a man's wife is his mother. (Think former presidents.) These innocent misperceptions impact in unspeakably powerful ways.

yesterday's cross to bear is today's trigger event:
a handful of real-life cases

My friend Nancy, forty-eight, is a personal manager in the music business and is constantly photographed with her clients. In Nancy's own words, "I got up every morning, looked in the mirror, and thought the woman I saw looked shitty. It couldn't be me, cause I looked *so* horrible. My trigger was seeing all these photos of myself in the trades. I couldn't bear to be photographed anymore. Then I saw you backstage at the Letterman show after your facelift and thought, my God, there's hope. You looked natural and just like yourself but revitalized. And it was only three weeks after you'd had the surgery. I knew then it would just be a matter of time for me."

It took Nancy five months to find the right moment. Her lift airbrushed her face back to what it had been at thirty-five. Her mother is thrilled, her boyfriend is puffing with pride, and a series of younger men concoct excuses for business meetings. In the past, Nancy was squeamish about the tiniest sight of blood. Today she is more beautiful than she was in her youth, and enlightened about her own personal strength. In spite of her fears, she was the best healer I've seen yet.

Another friend is an adored alcoholic who returned from a reha-bilitation clinic restored internally to her natural joy and wit. But physically she had been obviously (in horse lingo) "rode hard and put up wet." She wanted to minimize the evidence of her years of self-abuse and felt nothing short of a facelift would be effective. Anna was right. She looked ten years fresher and, after a few months, got her original job back—something no one would have thought possible, starting with her boss. In Anna's case cosmetic surgery was an extension of forgiving herself and getting back on the carousel—of wearing not a hair shirt, but merely her restored face. She had cared enough to repair the external damage as well, though she had to pay for it on an installment plan.

Everyone can think of a husband who has split for a younger model. And our reaction is generally a function of whether we identify with the Wife or her Replacement. *Self* magazine has pointed out that if you think a facelift can save a relationship, there are two special words for you: "Ivana Trump." *Self* is right, to some degree. I suspect, however, that Ms. Trump's surgery helped rescue her self-esteem from those belittling years with The Donald—and I'm willing to bet it's had a lot to do with her fantastic successes since.

Mary Lee's case is remarkable. During her college years she was an extrovert, a cheerleader, and a university spokesperson. She even married the man she loved. But when Mary Lee was twenty-seven, her brother's wife died very young, and raising his young children fell largely to her. At the same time, both her parents were diagnosed with terminal illnesses; the job of being their nurse/caretaker was added to her duties. Through these years she held down her job as an office manager. When her parents finally died, she emerged from an extended period of sadness and isolation at forty-seven. She saw the tension and grief of those years etched on her face, and she determined somehow to leave her cocoon and find herself again.

Within the year, Mary Lee had a facelift, her only cosmetic surgery, and enrolled in a modeling course to see if she could regain her former poise. The waiting room at the modeling school began to fill with ". . . these gorgeous long, lean kids in their teens and twenties," and Mary Lee wanted to flee. Still, she made herself finish the course, during which she was spotted by an agent as a perfect model for the "petite/mature" slot. Her self-esteem and joy had been lost in years of grieving, and suddenly her life was again filled with activity and work.

In her own words, "I discovered what I was looking for, which was me—back in my twenties just before everything stopped. I quit looking haggard and exhausted. I began to look fresh and feel excited about life. I realized I could do something and that made me whole again." It's been several years, and she's still an extremely successful model based in Knoxville, Tennessee. Her life is filled with friends, many of whom are younger, and she travels quite a bit. The facelift was her vehicle.

Then there's Miranda and Ginny, twins separated at birth. Miranda spent decades trying to locate her sister who, like her, had been adopted. At fifty-two, she finally succeeded in making phone contact. The women agreed to meet in Texas eight weeks later so they'd be able to coordinate vacations. Ginny lived in an area where sun exposure was part of daily life, and she intuited that her life had been more difficult than her sister's. Convinced she would look much older than her twin, she found a plastic surgeon and proceeded to schedule a mini-lift. Unfortunately, when she met her sister, Ginny hadn't healed from her surgery as much as she'd hoped. But no problem . . . Miranda had had her own facelift the year before, and they spent their first hour together comparing lifts—infinitely more pressing than discussing the past forty years.

From my own research, I believe the great majority of facelifts are triggered by:

- *a woman's leaving a marriage of significance (not an eighteen-month romp) due to either death or divorce*
- *a woman's effort to protect her position in a youth-oriented career market*
- *a woman's courting or being married to a much younger man*
- *a woman's suddenly discovering the deterioration of her jawline, neck, and jowls (frequently she will be totally unaware of what has slipped in her mid-face area)*
- *a woman (or man's) utter vexation over feeling younger than she/he looks.*

early effects of a trigger event

The short-term effects of a Trigger Event are intense anxiety and horror, which quickly collapse into a phase of grave self-examination. The Trigger may have been harsh in delivery (they are never fun), and a reevaluation of self-image results. At emotional gunpoint, we tiptoe into the minefield, attempting to pick up the trail where we left it years ago. I coasted along ten years overtime, vaguely presuming that because I felt thirty-five, I might still compute as that age. Lunacy on my part. The fact was, I had quit counting. Suddenly it became more urgent than breathing to scrutinize the remains and assess my damage—from facial liver spots, canyons, furrows, and bulges, to charred and slackened skin. In the reflection of a triple magnifying mirror, I removed the veil from my eyes and traced with my finger what had lapsed from cheekbone to chin.

Denial dies incredibly hard. How had I missed the landslide? I had fallen asleep at the wheel.

To my surprise, I was not alone. Within weeks, dozens of friends and acquaintances were confessing their growing consternation over *this one fact:* Each had come to deplore the fact that she was *looking* older than she felt.

the fork in the road

Once enlightened, I had to determine whether I possessed the maturity to let things continue their downslide or whether I was ready to begin shopping for surgical salvation. Whether I was secure enough to feel valued exactly as I was, and whether failing to pursue cosmetic surgery might cost me my lifestyle or career. For many individuals in the public eye, this last issue is a serious one. In such cases, cosmetic surgery might almost be considered a legitimate business expense. Not being a CEO, broadcaster, spokesperson, or actress, however, the decision for me had to be purely personal. The choice between stoicism and surgery was easy. I was certainly not secure enough to fly in the face of gravity and oxidation.

Safely past the Julia Roberts stage, I imagined for a moment who my husband might rave about next—and rapidly concluded that if the damage were fixable, I'd be an ass not to give it a try.

I started saving money immediately. Only if I had been an accomplished scientist, an important political figure, a devout feminist, or a nun, would I have chosen to tough it out. After all, the physical facts of life could only deteriorate from their present state.

how old do i have to be?

Needing a facelift means different things for different people. Doctors themselves disagree on what general age is ideal. Harvard's Dr. Robert Goldwyn is disturbed by the perceived trend toward early facelifts. He contends that not only will the scars be thicker on a patient in her forties, but the likelihood for sequential lifts becomes higher. Dr. Pat Maxwell, among many others, now believes it is clear the best results are achieved on younger patients— due to the elasticity of younger skin and longer-lasting results. He is generally supportive of the patient who strongly feels she could benefit from a facelift—regardless of her age and whether it is broadly agreed that she "needs" it.

In the past, facelifters cracked their closet doors and tiptoed to their surgeons somewhere after fifty and before seventy-five. By today's standards, at forty-seven, I was late to step in line. Fresh jargon is used in the consult now. For example, *chronological* age is passé and biological age is the new marker, with its non-specificity occasionally letting us off the hook. You may have the legs and wrinkles of a thirty-year-old, while your chins are mounting up and your brow has drooped. So, much as we may welcome the less conventional marker, it forces us to consider other reasons for our physical deterioration, ones that could be even more brutal—determined by genetics, sun damage, stress, smoke exposure, drug history, booze history, and other self-abusive lapses.

What this translates to is now you must own up to however

prematurely bad you may look, whether it's congenital or induced by unwise behavior. You may have decent grounds to get
your eyes done at thirty-two. Or order an injection to freeze your
squinting (forehead) muscles at twenty-five, if bad vision makes
you strain and wrinkles are etching in. Your age no longer decides
it. Whenever it bothers you is when you are "allowed" to get it
fixed. And never before in history has such a wide selection of
cosmetic fixes been available to everyone. As Dr. Steven Hoefflin
sees it, "The patients of today are very appearance conscious,
evaluate themselves for surgery starting in their thirties, and want
facelifts at a much earlier age."

There are dozens of ways to medically airbrush an aging face.
They are for sale right now, and cheap. The fact is, the lure of
cosmetic improvement is entirely cross-cultural, no longer re-
served for the rich. Some techniques are simple, some are more
involved. For the man or woman in the public eye (who must
calculate the future value of his or her face) these procedures are a
way of life. And relative youth is no disqualifier. In fact, *preventive*
cosmetic work is the buzz of the aesthetic cognoscenti.

> *Your face is your window to the world. Thousands of*
> *interactions and assumptions are based on your face, the one*
> *thing others can see.*
>
> —Dr. Jack Fisher

During the last twenty years, cosmetic surgery has become increasingly available to anyone seriously interested. It became a

retail commodity as the Boomer generation bloomed. Their credo seems to be, "Live well, have stylish things, stay pretty, and never fall into the spiraling demise of body and spirit we watched our parents endure." This generation comes with a stunning sense of entitlement, which, even more stunningly, seems to work. The White House and the majority of congressional seats are filled with kids whose aspirations were shaped by the lyrics of Disney's old TV theme song, "When You Wish Upon a Star." This group has refused to lose the zest for life into which it was (post-war) born. And the old attitudes took a beating from which they never sprang back. (For example, one must not wear long hair after forty; white shoes are forbidden after Labor Day; a lady never wears red; and wear fine underwear anytime you leave the house—in case an accident delivers you onto a hospital examining table.)

beautiful people never confess

The average American woman perceives television personalities to be realistic representatives of their stated age. Unfairly, she gauges herself to be a total shlump compared to, say, Cybill Shepherd, Candice Bergen, or Jaclyn Smith. The reason is: *Perennially beautiful people don't give away their secrets,* an unspoken but universal policy. This includes *any* celebrity, and often women noted for their sequential marriages. These people lie like dogs. They bat their eyes and claim they drink spinach juice and do stretches every day. Or that their particular guru affords them serenity to reverse their aging. Farrah Fawcett credits her current appearance to the daily sit-ups she made into a habit when "Charlie's Angels" was the rage. *Clue:* When an actress expounds on her trainer and an agonizing diet, what she's really had is serious body-sculpting lipo (possibly on her neck and chin also), at least a browlift, and a grand series of peels. And the farther she is past forty, the more likely she's had a facelift—one, at the very least.

Most leading models are lovely to start with, but they are exquisitely maintained by their surgeon and dermatologist. If they lean toward a unique look, a doctor with a good eye might accentuate that look by adding some tissue, making already nice features into unbelieveably striking ones. No one is as perfect as she may look on TV or in photos. Each one is a work in progress, and probably under the watchful eye of a doctor. Her surgeon understands the urgency for aesthetic perfection relative to his patient's career, and makes his adjustments very gradually. Not many plastic surgeons are inclined to work this way, though top models and actresses are often "made" by doctors who will. Generally speaking, these types are indigenous to Los Angeles.

> *Thirty-five is a very attractive age. London society is full of women of the very highest birth who have, of their own free choice, remained thirty-five for years.*
>
> —Oscar Wilde

Actors are endlessly youthful, spritely, and sparkly-eyed, seemingly immune to gravity's pull. But maintaining this lie requires a lot of help from the world of aesthetic surgeons. Beautiful people hope like hell we'll hang our heads in the face of their age-defying genes. Please do not. They have very skilled doctors who are taking a nip, tuck, or a lipo-suck every few years (or months!). A facelift at thirty in the Hollywood community isn't uncommon . . . so take it from there.

fifty today bears no resemblance to what fifty was ever before

Several years ago, I noticed everyone but me was flashing a blindingly beautiful smile. I was informed that its importance in first impressions could never be underestimated. I began to count, and realized that more women than I dreamed had scraped up the thousands required to buy exquisite teeth. I opted for the cheap way out and found a home bleaching kit for my uppers. It had never occurred to my parents or their friends to custom-order veneers before a significant birthday. Or to sneak in a browlift and a peel. Or spend one tenth of their annual income on clothing, coiffure, and shoes. All these developments are spin-offs of the modern stampede to market superficial goods that promise endless youth.

I've had a blessed life, for which I thank my parents. But anyone who's made it to forty-five has suffered some blows to the gut: deaths, sudden or slow, of family and friends; financial reverses; betrayals; and loss—the imperceptible creeping mantle of melancholy that comes with the passage of years. I knew it only too well, and like a slowly deflating inner tube, I was losing my joie de vivre. A situation that had to change.

The change in my face was only the tip of the iceberg. Fortunately, it didn't get alienized or shrunken. It simply got tidied up and restored to the way it was ten or five or fifteen years ago. But changes far more interesting than the facial ones also took place. To my shock, I felt restored to the mindset I'd had decades ago—the attitude that whatever barriers I ran up against, my job was to surmount them and go on from there. The results of the surgery were a blast of B_{12} to my sociability, withered confidence, and general level of energy.

Ironically, I felt freed from the mindset of apology about my appearance. I barely wore makeup, and I focused more on the people around me. What I'm trying to explain here isn't about vanity; it's more about middle-age freedom. God knows I'm not turning heads on the street, but I am doing the best with what I've got—or, to be precise, what I've got left. The surgery translated into an attitude boost that all the money on earth couldn't buy.

If I could dispense this feeling in pill form, I would do it, from every street corner in every town. Maybe it's coincidental, but I'm less distracted by all the static, and clearer about what's important to me. I don't understand it, but I'm grateful as hell.

> *Over the years, I have found that people who*
> *undergo successful cosmetic surgery develop*
> *a new view of themselves. The person lurking*
> *inside dares to come forth . . . and all of*
> *life seems to take on a new face.*
>
> —Dr. Tom Rees

it's never too late for a trigger event

- *A seventy-five-year-old woman went to Dr. Frank Kamer in Beverly Hills for the nose job she had wanted all her life. First her parents had objected, then her children, and finally she prevailed.*
- *A woman with a cleft lip for seventy-two years of her life decided one day to get it fixed. The doctor she chose, Debra Johnson of Sacramento, also did breast reconstruction on a seventy-nine-year-old woman who greatly enjoyed dressing up for Bingo night.*
- *An eighty-six-year-old woman with a younger man in hot pursuit asked Dr. Peter McKinney of Chicago for his best facelift. He graciously obliged.*
- *An eighty-five-year-old beauty, on the eve of her third marriage, had Dr. Craig Foster of New York City perform a third facelift to match.*
- *A recently lifted daughter in San Francisco took her eighty-five-year-old mother in to consult with her surgeon, Dr. Bruno Ristow. The mother followed her daughter's example and now looks twenty-five years younger, and has barely lost a hand of bridge since.*

Surgery on the elderly accomplishes personality changes in three hours, which the greatest psychoanalyst could not achieve.

—Dr. Anthony Napoleon

With the compilation of years, I'd begun entering rooms feeling apologetic, disqualifying myself from life's pulse. I could inversely gauge my self-esteem by the amount of make-up I wore. These days it's next to none. While it's not as if I look thirty, my need for a mask has diminished. I feel good in my recycled skin. An odd comfort it is, which eluded me in my nervous twenties when the cosmetic parts were intact.

Feeling better about yourself from successful surgery makes others around you happier and often improves work.

—Dr. Mark Gorney

2

making the
commitment

Do it early before you look shot.
A facelift around forty, a touch-up in your fifties, a browlift
in your seventies. It's the only way.

—an exquisitely beautiful Woman of the Theater

from childhood to twenty, I had rudely ignored Mama's thousand warnings to stay out of the midday sun. She was trying to preserve me for thirty years hence, but thirty minutes hence was the maximum I could project. I was certain to be less conventional and more courageous than she, and as such, unfazed by wrinkles or moles. Mama was old and could not comprehend I'd be impervious to these silly details. She also had not the vaguest idea how stubborn and stupid I was. From twenty to forty, in fact, I languished in the midday sun.

Redheads who overstay their welcome in the sun are the first in line to go. Liver spots, precancerous zones, freckles decades past their peak, and leathery skin at last made me take note. As one option, I could always do nothing and let my disintegration progress. Live with the miles of jellyfish moving in to blight the shore. Or I could take my best shot, discomfort aside, and pray for a midnight reprieve. Besides, life had just gotten great for me. But I needed information before I could make a decision. So suddenly I'm desperately craving the straight, cold facts about a facelift:

- The pros and cons (was it outrageously narcissistic?)
- How much would it hurt?
- How much time would I have to block out of my life?
- Was I a decent candidate for successful surgery?
- How insanely much would it cost?

I remember when my beauty routine consisted of three simple things: remembering to use moisturizer, staying a certain weight, and striving to keep a tan. Ultimately these things no longer worked, and neither did anything else. Moisturizer doesn't spread so well on skin that's basically seared. And the briefest exposure to sun now made my sunspots crack and bleed. Though trimness is somewhere near godliness, for the time-ravaged face, emaciation can add ten years.

As soon as I began to consider a facelift, I searched through several computer banks and many dozens of bookstores. I longed for a warts-and-all guide written in time-honored girltalk with a day-by-day description of what to expect. Nothing in Latin-based medical terms. More of a peek at Fran Drescher's diary, crammed with personal tips to coach me through. More than anything I wanted an Auntie Mame, who, with a wave of her cigarette holder, could keep the bad parts at bay and brace me for what was to come.

There are hundreds of books on plastic surgery out there, but I never found the one I wanted. The good news is, you have.

> *People don't mind growing up,*
> *they just don't want to look old.*
>   —Dr. Arnold Klein

A perfect window of time pops out of the calendar. My husband will be gone on a business trip and August in New York City sucks, so I see myself recovering in a cool pastel room with stacks of wonderful books, precisely when the elite and eagle-eyed will be vacationing hard at the beach. I tentatively decide to forge ahead, but I'm sickened with second thoughts. The pros and cons lope through my mind for weeks before I can sleep. Me arguing with me. Here's how it went:

Con: I don't know anyone who's had a facelift and will admit it, not to mention explain it to me. Maybe I should wait a few more years until I need it even more.

Pro: Are you nuts? That same reasoning stopped you three years ago. Look in the mirror and consider it maintenance. Make a preemptive strike before you're too old to enjoy the results.

Con: But a better person would give the same money to feed hungry children or train Seeing Eye dogs for the blind. How did I end up with such superficial values that I'm seriously considering a facelift? Was all this put in motion when Mama put braces on my teeth?

Pro: If you must look at it that way, yes. Mothers throughout history would have done the same thing. Not to mention if anesthesia had been around, Cleopatra would have been the Cher of her millennium. Decide now to be more generous in the future if guilt is a serious factor.

Con: It probably wouldn't work. Look at my friend Sooz. She's much older than I am and she looks fantastic. She even smoked for years and she's never had a doctor touch her face.

Pro: Don't be stupid. She always looked better and she's got better genes. Your facelift isn't about her.

Con: Fine. What if I die on the table?

Pro: Those odds are one in ten thousand. You're more likely to die in a car crash less than a mile from your home.

Con: God, I must be living a shallow life to be even thinking of this.

Pro: Of course you are, but it's too late now. Didn't you ever stuff your bra when you were a teenager, or try to lighten your hair with lemon juice? Go on and get the facelift—gravity doesn't take any holidays. Get off your tail and start the research.

Every culture is a beauty culture. I defy anyone to point to any society at any time in history or any place in the world, that wasn't preoccupied with beauty.

—Newsweek

If you're wrestling with the vanity issue, take a look around you. A viral profusion of painted hair reigns, even in little towns. The majority of women alter their shade, as do a growing number of men. Guys with bad dye jobs are everywhere. (Someone needs to clue them in to the fact that the monochromatic look isn't convincing.) Your plumber's probably using a rinse. And the business men you know are into conditioners, mousse, and minoxidil—and hiding hairspray under the seat of their car.

> *Anyone who has ever looked in a mirror*
> *or brushed their hair is a candidate.*
> —Dr. Alan Matarasso

First impressions always counted, but now they count more. Especially in the competitive workplace. Once it was background, education, and character. Now it's more how you look and what you've done lately. Studies even correlate financial success with physical attractiveness. Dr. Anthony Napoleon is a medical psychologist, forensic analyst, and leading authority on the analysis and implications of beauty. In his 1980 study, he discovered that psychiatric nurses and physicians were giving less severe diagnoses to patients who were better looking. He is endlessly knowledgeable and explains flatly, "The top [cosmetic] surgeons are doing psychiatry with a knife. The sad fact is, how we communicate is a function of how we perceive ourselves to look. Self-image is a clinical concept and attractiveness makes any commodity more marketable than ever before."

a view from abroad

Though plastic surgery is riotously embraced in Italy, France, and South America, the Brits have been slow to come around. Here is a fax from a friend in England, an actor, who puts his finger squarely on the United Kingdom's sentiments on the subject:

"It is, I'm afraid, a fact that the British regard plastic surgeons as being one rung on the evolutionary ladder below dung beetles. I don't know why this is. We regard hygiene (what you call 'freshness' I believe), depilation, and deodorants in the same light. Perhaps it's northern European guilt: If our lives have caused us to sag, wrinkle, and smell, then it would be wickedness to attempt to cover it up. Something like that. Even showbiz types who have a facelift are laughed at in the public prints. One of my friends is a Mediterranean beauty married to a Tory and gives facelifts as Christmas presents. Her English friends who receive these accept them happily, giving as their excuse that it would offend her not to have the work done. Since she's foreign, this legitimizes their delight in having what they secretly wanted anyway without losing their miserable English dignity."

—Stephen Fry

what exactly is a facelift?

Okay. A facelift is real surgery. It is nothing remotely like a lunchtime fix. Any person or article who indicates so would be lying through their teeth. However, the territory is carefully charted, and hundreds are performed every day. In 1994 and 1995, almost forty thousand facelifts were performed in the United States alone. Final facelift figures for 1996 are expected to be between sixty-seven and seventy thousand.

The facelift of the past simply evened the hem on a badly stretched-out skirt. Usually that hem didn't last very long, but it was a step in the right direction. Cosmetic surgery of this type, making excisions in strategic areas of facial skin, developed in Europe and America at approximately the same time.

One of the earliest attempts at a facelift was performed by Dr. Eugen Hollander of Berlin, in 1901, on a Polish aristocrat. The lady presented him with her own drawings, and though he was hesitant to perform such an operation, she used what he termed "feminine persuasion" to recruit him. She wanted certain strips of skin removed from various points close to her hairline, seemingly to lift wrinkles and sags. His attempt was successful, though the general technique seems archaic now and the results were not long-lasting. Dr. Hollander waited thirty years to publish a report of his work—probably because he feared the established medical community would disapprove of surgery done for mere cosmetic reasons. The history of plastic surgery is fascinating, and is immaculately chronicled by Dr. Blair O. Rogers in numerous articles that can be found at the New York Academy of Medicine Library.

Prior to World War I, Sir Harold Gillies of London was successfully performing reconstructive work on civilians in London. When the war began, he turned his talents to rehabilitating wounded soldiers and citizens. He made the first forays, and quite successfully, into plastic and reconstructive surgery, for which he was knighted in 1930. Following the war, Dr. Archibald McIndoe joined him in his practice, as Sir Harold expanded his talents to encompass cosmetic work as well. Sir Harold Gillies is considered the father of plastic surgery as we know it today.

Lifts today are a virtual art form and tackle the problem at deeper levels. The skin is opened and excess fat is delicately removed from the face, jawline, and neck (extirpating the years of mayo and buttered popcorn abuse we once subjected ourselves to). The hated, drain-clogging substance is chicken-fat yellow (unless you're a beta-carotene freak, in which case it's golden orange). Most doctors seem partial to one version or another of the SMAS (superficial musculoaponeurotic system) lift, though there are other methods. The SMAS, developed in the seventies and eighties, tightens muscles and tissues in the face and neck and removes extra fat from the neck and chin. Another facelift technique recycles the original fat (which may have slipped in the eye and cheek area) and restores it to its original position, while lifting corresponding muscles in the face as well. Doctors subscribing to this technique (such as Sam Hamra of Texas) are adamant about saving facial fat to fully re-create a youthful look. Ultimately, rigid adherence to one technique or another is less important than thoroughly assessing the individual face and providing each patient with a purely custom job. In doing so, aspects of several techniques might easily be incorporated into one facelift.

During the operation, the doctor's nurse works almost telepathically in concert with him, economizing on both movements and time. Having watched several surgeons at work, I consider it the highest marriage of art and science I've had the privilege to observe.

Beneath the skin, the muscles and connective tissue are tightened up so the skin can be redraped over cleaner, smoother contours, minus the old lumps and sags. When everything is sewn back up, you're rid of a lot of extraneous mess, and the planes of your face are cleaner. Any detritus is whisked away and the upholstery looks remarkably similar to the way it did years before.

At the turn of the last century, humans were lucky to survive to forty-five or fifty. Now that we routinely live well into our eighties, some maintenance and an occasional overhaul seem perfectly reasonable to me.

but why are people having facelifts?

Because they can. For the first time in history.

Humans always strived for cosmetic improvement and to maintain the illusion of youth. Now we have the tools to achieve these things—an arsenal of them in fact. Not to mention thousands of trained practitioners eager to do the work. By the the year 2000, cosmetic surgery may well be viewed as no more than a technological extension of makeup.

how do i know if i need it?

You absolutely might not need a facelift. In fact, the odds are you don't. If the improvement would be only marginal, wait until later on. It's similar to the way that balding men need to reach a certain plateau of hair loss before they move into the transplant stage. If your appearance isn't relevant to your passion or your work, don't give it another thought. You are blessed with the grace and wisdom to live with the signs of your age.

The rest of us might try these simple tests, which two highly respected surgeons use on hundreds of patients each year. The first one is the brainchild of Dr. Bruce Connell, who has an impeccable reputation, most especially for his work on men. His simple gauge is to place four fingers horizontally between your eyebrow and your hairline. If it takes more than four fingers to join these, you're probably looking old. (I've never seen this test fail.) Another one is favored by Dr. Harvey Zarem. He tells the woman who wants a consultation to lie back in a reclining chair and relax. While prone, she's given a hand mirror and asked to examine herself, noting especially the position of her brows. What she sees essentially, is how Dr. Zarem thinks she'll look six months after a lift. If she sees very little difference, he considers she doesn't yet need one. As Dr. Craig Foster might put it, "It's a long run for a short slide—the results you'd see aren't worth the procedure you're talking about." Zarem feels strongly that people often confuse a brow that's drooped with redundant eyelid skin, and assume they need eyelid surgery when a browlift is more to the point. Similarly, he cautions against perceiving a facelift as the panacea for all facial flaws. He would, by the way, prefer to operate on a recovered heart attack patient than on a secret drug user—the odds for the former may be better in terms of both survival and successful results.

only the truth . . .
how much will it hurt?

The thing you better know now is exactly how much it hurts. The answer varies, but here's the general idea: For a *pure facelift,* not very much. It is not stabbing pain and it is not a spinal tap. The nurses I have spoken to tell me only one in approximately twelve patients has anything more than *discomfort.* I know women who never reached for one pain pill, but it must be said that the effects of anesthesia last long after the surgery is done. Dr. Susan Craig Scott, whose specialty is lifts and eyes, contends that pain should not even be part of the memory. She encourages early use of pain medication so discomfort can be largely avoided. When you get past the first three days, the discomfort should steadily decline, but you won't feel resilient right away. Your wound is trying to heal itself, so rest and give it some help.

Here are a few testimonials on the issue of facelift pain:

"Mine was totally without pain. The whole thing was more of an inconvenience than anything else. For a few weeks I was terrified to make any rapid movements for fear of pulling an interior stitch. On a discomfort scale from one to ten, I'd say it was a two." [She had a facelift only.]

"I had a facelift thirty years ago in London and it was nothing. I ate a green apple that night, and have had two more facelifts since." [This case is unusual.]

"I didn't have any pain, I just wasn't quite well. I never took a pain pill but once—and that was over my apprehension about having the early stitches removed. So it was cheating in a way, anticipating pain that didn't exist. I felt so fragile, like I was recovering from a car wreck. And I believe the grogginess of the anesthesia works in your favor the first few days. Discomfort level? Occasionally it was a six but not usually." [Facelift only.]

"The whole thing was nothing. I was under anesthesia or sleeping or on pain-killers and I never did feel bad. Watching me recover was more painful for my wife than for me." [Male, fifty years old, facelift and some pot-belly liposuction.]

what does it cost in time?

How long before you're back at the office or having a bite with a friend? Down time will always depend on:

* *how much surgery you're having done at one time (a lift only, or the addition of numerous bells and whistles, known as "ancillary procedures"). You might also be having breast reduction and some*

body contouring at the same time. The more procedures you com-
bine, the longer the recovery will take—and probably the worse
you'll feel. On the other hand, if you're planning to have a number
of procedures, combining them can save you from sequential sur-
geries.

• *whether or not you're capable of following post-op instructions. Will*
you rest, take your medicines, and follow your instruction sheet all
the way? Or will you feel a burning need to do some laundry, push
the vacuum around, rearrange kitchen cabinets, and have a drink at
the end of the day? Straining yourself at crucial healing stages can
blow everything you've done. It can even be life-threatening, depend-
ing on how careless you get.

• *luck. Luck includes your skin type and genetic history, which you*
hope will not predispose you to complications. It also involves the
quality of your general health when you go into surgery, the skill of
the doctor you choose, and the underlying state of your life. Flexibil-
ity and an upbeat attitude will help more than you might suspect.

more specifically . . .

If you go for a straight facelift, you might be at the movies four or
five days later, hidden beneath your sunglasses and a scarf. The
first two or three days won't be great, but at the end of the week
you'll feel better. At ten days you'll be lurking around your home
or neighborhood, and thrilled by what you're starting to see. By
two weeks, you'll be well on the mend, encouraged daily by your

results. Somewhere between two and three weeks after, you'll be back to your normal routine. The more frills you add to your lift, the more areas will have to heal, so your recovery won't be as quick.

will a facelift work for me
or will i be sorry?

Roadside Warning: Some people are poor facelift candidates. It won't be your age that disqualifies you, but it might be your motivation. If you recognize yourself in the following profiles, think twice before you go for a consultation—you could save yourself a lot of money and time. Any experienced surgeon has done thousands of consultations and is trained to listen for little indicators that having surgery won't deliver your fix. He will be hipper to this than you will, so don't try to fake him out. Remember, he gets paid to operate, so it's probably you he's trying to protect.

If, for example, your interest in surgery is triggered by one looming occasion—your husband's planning his retirement, or your son's getting married in June—it might not be ideal. Sometimes the aftereffects of the perceived event are what's really stuck in your throat. Surgery can't solve that for you. Take a nap or get some sleep and dream about what underpinnings your life could *really* use. Remember, you can have a lift until you're ninety, so don't fix what you didn't break.

• • •

In the privacy of your heart, determine whose idea this was, and *don't do it for someone else.* Let's say your mother primed you to be a dancer but you longed to be an engineer. Again, you can waste a lot of money and time, but in the end it won't work. A lift will not make your boyfriend come back, drive a stake through your rival's heart, or get your boss to give you a raise. The lift must be for yourself alone (this can mean your inner self, your outer self, or your future self—the one you're trying to free). Any other reason puts you on very shaky ground. Would you marry someone because your brother likes him and thinks it's a good idea? Or gain fifteen pounds because your grandmother worries you're too thin to fight off disease? Getting a facelift is no different. The premise is exactly the same. Don't let anyone persuade or pressure you. Tell anyone who is pushing you that you'll do it when *you're* ready. Maybe by then they'll be out of your life.

Now focus on your expectations. If you believe your facelift will make you twenty-five again, please hear this: It won't. Nothing will. If the improvements your doctor anticipates from surgery would be only marginal, wait a little longer. An honorable doctor who suggests waiting has no ulterior motive—just vastly broader experience than you have. If you hope to come out looking like Michelle Pfeiffer and you go in as Rosie O'Donnell, surgery isn't a good idea. If you look almost like Ms. Pfeiffer's double and want one feature fixed . . . well sure. Otherwise your goal is not achieveable, and any approximation of success would involve multiple operations. At the end of which you still might be disappointed.

two case histories

Dot and Millie are contemporaries. They have similar jobs in different cities, each of which demands substantial interaction with the public. Both have significant sun damage and extra flesh under the chin. Millie is eighteen months past her divorce, and Dot is trying to breathe life into her marriage. Millie has been reassigned to the headquarters she left ten years ago and looks forward to being reunited with her old cohorts. She inquires about a facelift because she's becoming less comfortable in public and she'd like to start fresh when she moves, both socially and on the job.

Dot's husband has been unfaithful for several years. She feels that he has not been attracted to her since they both turned forty-five. He once loved her face, and she's convinced that a facelift will restore the original glow to her marriage. She is anxious and weeping during the consultation, and desperately hopes the doctor will comply.

Who is the better candidate for a successful facelift? In the doctor's view, Dot's reasoning is totally inappropriate, and her results are likely to disappoint her. As he commented, "The guy may come home for lunch for a few weeks, but it's not going to fix the marriage." Millie is the better candidate. Her expectations are more realistic. Dot is lingering in a state of denial and looking the wrong way for help. She's headed for more disappointment, and in her misery would prefer to blame anyone but the right person, her husband. Until she has no choice. Her case is loaded with warning flags.

more bad candidates
for elective surgery:
(facelift certainly included)

- *hemophiliacs, and victims of von Willebrand disease, Christmas disease, or any other bleeding disorder*
- *pregnant women*
- *anyone who has been recently obese*
- *anyone just released from drug rehab*
- *anyone in a state of emotional turmoil*
- *any woman who has suffered a recent miscarriage*
- *anyone who is paranoid or depressed*
- *anyone who continues to smoke.*

Dr. Mark Gorney created an acronym to help him identify a certain sector of bad candidates during the interview. From years of experience, he has determined that patients who are

> S: single
> I: immature
> M: male, eighteen to forty years old
> O: overexpectant
> N: narcissistic

have a higher likelihood of having problems with cosmetic surgery. He provided me with the following example:

A twenty-five-year-old male, an aspiring actor, came in about a rhinoplasty. He felt he had a nose that limited him to "Shylock" parts. It had always disturbed him, so the surgeon took him on. He did an excellent job on the man, but as soon as the bandages were removed, the patient became hysterical, exclaiming, "My nose, my nose, my beautiful nose. . . . What have you done to me?"

On his next visit to the office the patient brought his girl friend, who liked the job and asked to see the doctor alone. The problem, she explained, was that her beau was a poor actor, and the doctor had just removed his crutch. It was a lesson for the doctor that the motive of the patient must be carefully assessed, and the risk/benefit ratio expertly determined.

good candidates for a facelift

- *people who have the flexibility to deal with life's imperfections*
- *people who are realistic, who know Mother Nature is always in charge, and doctor, staff, and patient (however superb) can only do their best*
- *people with reasonable expectations of the surgical result*
- *people who are not essentially angry or unhappy*
- *people who have a rapport with and trust in their physician.*

*there is no surgery
to make a sad person happy
or erase an abusive past.*

We all have to be very cautious of the insatiable patient.
—Dr. Stanley Klatsky

cash on the barrelhead?

If you are a good candidate and have decided to pursue a lift, there's still the glum subject of cost to be considered—since payment's usually due in advance. Once only movie stars and heiresses could afford cosmetic surgery. For years they would jet to Brazil for several weeks on the private island of Dr. Ivo Pitanguy. His gift in this field is legendary, and internationally he was long known as the world's best-known plastic surgeon. But to be his patient you had to go to Brazil and be there for some time. Hence, he was largely taking care of the Western world's Café Society, as well as international stars. But Pitanguy determined that he could ultimately make his healing art available to the poor and injured as well.

Through Dr. Pitanguy's efforts, recent scientific advances, and the pleas of a clamoring market, the cost has now dropped to the point where cosmetic surgery is affordable for virtually everyone. An aerobics teacher, a paralegal, a schoolteacher, and the governor's wife could easily meet in the doctor's waiting room with no one having a clue about the other's life or economic circumstances. (For those who prefer not to be seen, private entrances and waiting rooms are usually an option to be arranged in advance on the phone.)

Still pressing for a dollar amount?

Okay.

Anywhere from $2,000 to $25,000. The average surgeon's fee

for a facelift in the United States was $4,293 in 1994. This figure will vary from one city to another, generally depending on operating overhead and what reputation the doctor may have established. The most costly cosmetic surgery is done in California and New York. Probably next are Miami and Dallas. New York surgeons seem to charge between $7,000 and $15,000 for a facelift—which probably won't include a browlift or any work on your eyes. The surgeon's fee, however, isn't all. There's more. The costs of

- thorough pre-op examinations
- the use of the operating facility
- the anesthesiologist's fee (if it's not included with the surgeon's)
- an overnight stay in the hospital or in a medically supervised recovery facility

bump up the price 25 to 30 percent. The rule of thumb is that large urban centers equal higher overhead, costs, and fees. Plus the surgeon who has earned a brilliant reputation over a number of years might cost more than the new guy on the block. He also is probably worth it, if you happen to have the cash. So, to pick a round number, if the surgeon charges $10,000, the additional costs will bring the total close to $13,000. Very fine doctors are scattered all around the country, and you should definitely see more than one.

Although occasionally a drooping eyelid gets by as an actual visual threat, most cosmetic procedures are very rarely covered by insurance. Because of this, the custom is usually to pay up front. Sometimes financing can be worked out, and even credit cards are accepted, but many scheduled procedures have been scotched in favor of replacing a crumbling chimney, scheduling a family trip, dealing with tuition, or paying taxes. Aesthetic surgery is the first thing to go in a financial crunch. Curiously though, the same person in the same crunch might lease new cars each year or shell out a fortune for clothes.

The people on this list turned fifty in 1996. You decide if any of these people have had surgery yet . . .

Diane Keaton	*Sally Field*
Naomi Judd	*Marianne Faithful*
Sylvester Stallone	*Barry Manilow*
Linda Ronstadt	*Ron Silver*
Pat Sajak	*Lesley Ann Warren*
Suzanne Somers	*Gregory Hines*
Dolly Parton	*Michael Ovitz*
Cher	*Susan Saint James*

. . . or *if any have abstained.*

The people on this list turn fifty in 1997. What's your guess?

Jane Curtin	*Emmylou Harris*
Kareem Abdul-Jabbar	*Kevin Kline*
MeatLoaf	*Steven Spielberg*

Gregg Allman

Ry Cooder

Jaclyn Smith

Danny Glover

P. J. O'Rourke

Farrah Fawcett

Sam Neill

Arnold Schwarzenegger

David Letterman

Peter Weller

Chris Wallace

The confluence of beauty, wealth, and power is a universal phenomenon. Literally, it pays to be beautiful.
—Dr. Robert Goldwyn

The younger the face, the better the results. I love to see a lift done in the late thirties and early forties.
—Dr. James Baker

a supposed alternative: the "acupuncture facelift"

In China, women historically have gone to doctors for health reasons and left with cosmetic benefits. I can't speak from personal experience about this approach, but it does have some devoted followers. The "acupuncture lift" takes place over six months, with only one session a week. Traditionally it has been sought for treatment of chronic physical problems, such as lower back problems, headaches, poor circulation, sleep disorders, or recurring pain. After an assessment, the doctor chooses twelve or more Chinese herbs from the hundreds commonly used, and prescribes them as a tea. He recommends the tea as a daily supplement to the weekly sessions of acupuncture. Within three weeks, Dr. Bíao Lu, of Santa Monica, California, claims he sees improvement in digestion, circulation, sleeping habits, color, and absorption of nutrients.

Dr. Lu admits he cannot produce the overnight results of traditional surgery, but he feels that surgery fails to address the internal problems. In his view, women come for health reasons and leave with cosmetic benefits. Facial improvement is a side effect of "the overall treatment." The cost is $60 per week, plus the cost of the herbs. The entire process is under $2,000.

Most esteemed doctors in the United States dismiss this treatment as bunk. I, myself, am devoutly interested in alternative medical approaches, but I suspect the "acupuncture lift" may possibly be a misnomer for the "circulation booster."

I've known one of Dr. Lu's patients for twenty years, and her "acupuncture facelift" is worth a few words. She currently looks better than she has in years. Her face looks healthier and brighter, but lacks the precise improvements seen in a surgical lift. The areas unaffected by Dr. Lu are her eyes (needles can't get too close) and her neck, though she expects improvement still to come. Whether her refreshed face is the result of acupuncture or a change in her habits, I will never know.

final preparations

I decided, finally, to conserve any vestiges of my puritanical guilt for other occasions. Once I found the right doctor and my lift was scheduled, we had one final talk. I didn't want to look like a stranger, just tidied up to be my old self. The one I had been so careless with, broiled in the sun, and didn't deserve anymore. He is as honorable a man as I know, with an unfailing artistic eye. (Plastic surgeons, you may find, are often sculptors or artists on the side.) I asked him to please evaluate me a second time once the surgery was under way. I begged him to take absolute license to tackle anything with a chance to be restored, even if we hadn't discussed it in advance. I realized I might wake up to a bigger bill if there were added bells and whistles, but I also knew this was a one-shot deal and I'd better shoot for the moon. I figured in for a penny, in for a pound—and lucky to be in at all.

Though I was ripe for the kill, you might easily wrestle with this decision longer and from many serious points of view. The latest word, however, is to start young, cover all the little stuff, and stay one step ahead of your sags. Good news if you're still in your thirties, but I was too far gone for the little stuff. It was facelift or bust.

Over the years, I have found that people who undergo successful cosmetic surgery develop a new view of themselves. The person lurking inside dares to come forth . . . and all of life seems to take on a new face.

—Dr. Tom Rees

3
searching for
dr. right

The best results will be on someone who started early, maintained often, and kept up with it. Say, late thirties, early forties. Do it on the early side and you'll heal very well. Every five to seven years a little scar removal, skin adjustment. . . . Someone coming to the surgeon for the first time in her seventies may need two or three procedures.

—Dr. Peter McKinney

i am strangely apt to imbue all doctors with brilliance, dedication, and an overwhelming need to assist mankind. And plastic surgeons, as a group, I find to be competent, gregarious, artistic, excellent communicators, and passionate about their work. Reconstructive work is part of any practice, and includes correcting certain birth defects or scars, rebuilding body parts that have been traumatized by injury, and even reattaching severed body parts. Obviously these procedures make an enormous difference in the quality of a patient's life, and are, therefore, especially gratifying for the doctor. Most plastic surgeons enjoy their work, take it very seriously, and feel very rewarded to see each good result.

Sleazy, unskilled doctors do exist.

> *There are plenty of doctors I wouldn't let do*
> *hemorrhoids on my dog.*
>
> —Dr. Mark Gorney

Plastic surgery is the last medical specialty impervious to the restrictions of managed care; therefore, it's an appealing choice for those primarily interested in making money, and who may have little regard for a patient's results or future. But such doctors are by far in the minority, and sidestepping them requires only a little homework on your part—such as researching the surgeon's credentials carefully and meeting with satisfied patients.

begin with your friends

The ideal way to arrive at Dr. Right's door is by word of mouth. If you already know two or three women (the more the better) who have used the same surgeon and are happy with their results and their treatment as a patient, make this guy first on your list. In the event that you know women who have had cosmetic surgery but are not likely to admit it, simply ask them who they've *heard* is the best plastic surgeon around. Surely they'll tell you at least that much.

By the way, *do* start a list and don't lose it. Naturally, if you notice several women who look as if they come from a closely related colony of space aliens, maybe their doctor is not for you. Still, do ask the alien babes who they recommend, but consider him with caution.

Surprisingly, some of the strangest, most distorted looks are patient induced. That is, the patient herself requests the taut, caught-in-a-wind-tunnel look, and will have a more natural look revised until she achieves it. My point is that no one's responsible for Michael Jackson but himself. I wonder how many surgeons he ran through to get the skeletal look he has today.

Fifty percent of the consultation is screening the patient.
—Dr. Craig Foster

Even if you're certain which doctor you will use, you still need to educate yourself. This is no time to be frugal, thinking you'll save money by having only one consultation. That would be the equivalent of walking to the closest used-car dealer to buy a car because it's cheaper than spending the cab fare to go to an honest one.

ask your g.p.

Another source of good information should be your regular physician. Ask him or her to recommend two or three doctors—and see them all. If for some unfathomable reason you have reached facelift age and have no doctor, maybe you need to find a general practitioner before signing on for any cosmetic work. Another source for plastic surgeons would be the largest hospital in your county or region. Call and ask the hospital's administrative office for their Physicians Referral List of Board Certified Plastic Surgeons. Then add those names to your list. Hospital administration offices generally love to give you information.

board certification is crucial

When a surgeon is *board certified*, it means:

- He has graduated from an accredited medical school.
- He has completed three or more years as a resident in general surgery or its equivalent.
- He has undergone at least two years of approved training in plastic surgery.
- He has been a practicing physician for at least two years.
- He has passed extensive written and oral exams.
- He has been judged to meet the high ethical standards of the American Board of Plastic Surgeons.

Board certified doctors have earned their credentials and should be considered your best bet. There are some rare exceptions, but, generally speaking, being board certified is analogous to being a licensed driver. You wouldn't hire someone to drive you over a mountain range if you knew he didn't have a license, even though he might be the most skillful guy who ever sat behind a wheel, but for some quirky reason never bothered to take the test. As such, he would be the extremely rare exception.

Now we must zoom in on the specialty in which he is board certified.

Never go to a doctor's office whose plants have died.
—Erma Bombeck

accept no stand-in for a bcps

Anyone with a degree from medical school (with or without board certification) can legally attempt to perform plastic surgery. He may even be board certified—*just not in the specialty you need.* Remember the specialties? Pediatrics, ophthalmology, radiology, pathology, dermatology, psychiatry, etcetera? Be sure you're clear on this: In *which* specialty is he board certified? Your basic radiologist can take intensive "weekend courses" in liposuction, dermabrasion, peel techniques, and laser. He may not have the experience to recognize or handle any complications, and he will probably lack the ability to screen out patients who won't get satisfactory results. Still, he is technically kosher to take a stab at it and might ultimately become skilled—after he has most likely learned at the expense of innumerable patients. Any way you cut it, it's less risky to find a physician who is *board certified in plastic surgery.*

Never undertake a procedure unless you can handle
any related complications.

—Dr. Joel Kassimir

So fine, I sound like your mother. The reason is, a BCPS has had six to eight years' more training in plastic surgery than is required, so he won't be the guy who moonscaped your friend's thigh then punctured her skin with a laser—or at least the odds are way lower. You owe it to your body to do at least this much homework. This is no time to get lazy.

use the resources at hand

After trying doctor or patient referrals, you should phone the American Society of Plastic and Reconstructive Surgeons. This is another excellent source, reachable by dialing 1 (800) 635-0635. They will provide you with a list of five board certified plastic surgeons practicing near where you live, each of whom has made a commitment to continuing his medical education in three-year cycles. This is especially relevant in a field advancing so rapidly. The ASPRS has close to 4,500 members.

A second organization, the American Society of Aesthetic Plastic Surgery, is even more exclusive, and its members are primarily focused on the cosmetic aspects of plastic surgery. These surgeons pass exhaustive tests, are devoted to raising the standard for cosmetic surgery, and are admitted based on the quality of their work. No candidate is even considered until he has been in practice for three years *after* receiving his board certification. ASAPS has a toll-free number, 1 (888) 272-7711) you can call for information regarding its 1,251 members. ASAPS also has a web site that offers information on the various cosmetic procedures and a geographical roster of members. The ASAPS web site address is: http://surgery.org.

the unofficial route

Last, your long shot. Though this method is not conventionally approved, I have a feeling it works very well. Find the largest teaching hospital near you. Call there confidently, and ask for the name of the chief surgical resident (and when that person is available by phone). This individual should be familiar with the work of all the doctors practicing in his hospital, and will be able to assess their levels of skill. Courteously explain that you're an ignoramous; tell him you want the best facelift possible; ask him whose work he respects most and whom he would recommend (and if possible, in what order.) Add these names, then review your list, and look for any names that show up more than once. Make these your first consultations. A few doctors do not charge for consultations but most do. That fee can be anywhere from $50 to $250. Consider it the price of entry.

a few warning signs

According to Dr. Robert Goldwyn at Harvard, 43 percent of referrals come from other patients, 41 percent come from other doctors, and 8 percent from advertising in the yellow pages. Which brings us to the subject of advertising at all.

Presumably you are looking for skilled, trusted hands to address your face surgically—not a blacksmith or someone to get the wart off your son's foot. If you get lazy and let your first interview schmooze you into the O.R., you might be wearing the sloppy results on your face for the rest of your life.

Historically, advertising in the field of medicine has been frowned upon and considered suspect. Although doctor advertising has been legalized in the United States since the seventies, it still carries a stigma. Although some would disagree, I have great reservations about the plastic surgeon who advertises. It seems that instead of building up a solid practice by word of mouth, he is trying a shortcut that may in fact increase his overhead. In my view, advertising would indicate that he is a doctor just starting out (who may have fine training but comparatively little experience), or one with a fading practice. And yes, I'm sure there are some exceptions. But I would consider with some skepticism the doctor who wants to skip the time necessary to build up a reputation: It's possible that he didn't go into this with the best motives. In all likelihood, he may have invested heavily in an ad campaign.

All too frequently these ads skew the facts, list phony credentials or the doctor's membership in fictitious medical societies (we can all think of four or five letters to jumble up). Worst of all, he's got a big overhead to pay (the ad agency or its equivalent as well as the cost of the space or air-time), plus his operating expenses. This guy will be far less likely to turn away a patient—whether she actually needs surgery or not. He may even persuade her to undergo more surgery than she originally asked about. Aristotle addressed this issue centuries ago when he said, "It is not part of a physician's business to use either persuasion or compulsion upon the patient."

Be triply cautious of promises or guarantees made by either a doctor or an ad. If you're in a "promiser's" office, you'd be better off asking your veterinarian for a lift—he may be equally skilled and certainly more honest. There are no guarantees in life, re-member? This includes any surgery involving the human body—still the uncontested domain of Mother Nature.

If you are a person of color, you should also confirm that any surgeon you are considering is experienced in working with your skin type and knowledgeable about its particular complications. Ask to see before and after pictures of patients with your pigmen-tation and quirks. If he's only worked on blondes, keep searching and asking questions. The right doctor will be around the corner, or at worst two towns away.

tips from a malpractice lawyer
to save you from needing one

1. *Be cognizant of the full spectrum of risks, especially as they pertain to your individual medical history and that of your family.*
2. *Get an accurate figure on the doctor's rate of success for the intended procedure.*
3. *Know in advance what follow-up procedure might be required, if any.*
4. *Always get a second opinion, especially on good news.*
5. *Know who your anesthesiologist is and speak with him in person.*
6. *Know exactly what range of post-op support your doctor or his staff provides.*
7. *If a facial nerve were severed (granted this is rare), who would pay for the cost of reanimation surgery?*
8. *You already know this: Regardless of what anyone says, there are no guarantees.*

—Daniel Thomas, esq.
New York City

The basic premise is this:

You don't need to be hit with any surprises
once surgery day rolls around.
Nor, for that
matter, does your doctor.

the vital stuff

Now that we're done with the necessary formalities, let's move swiftly to the personal and irrational aspects. (To do this, try to assume temporarily that all the doctors on your list are equally talented.) Since facial rejuvenation is cosmetic by nature (that is, governed by aesthetics), consider no detail of apparel or decor too superficial. In fact, superficial is the name of the game—backed up by excellent credentials.

A doctor's office decor makes a subtle statement about who he means to be addressing—and, indeed, who he is himself. The furnishings, color tones, seating arrangements, and art are specific choices he's made, which should logically reflect his aesthetics. Every minute feature counts: colors, music, wall hangings (one waiting room I visited was plastered with framed letters from happy patients . . .), objets d'art, window treatments, wallpaper, and bookshelves. Even murals, and if so, of what? A mural can tell the whole story. If there are actually books on his shelves, what are the titles? Are any of them books you'd be interested in, or are they the handbooks of a flake, bought at rummage sale for decorative purposes? Are any of them books you wish you had read or intend to read again? This would be a positive sign. His pre-med education will probably be reflected here. See if your interests mesh.

Now, envision a room you consider to be aggressively "tacky." Is it similar to Roseanne's TV living room or a suite in the Four Seasons Hotel? How does *this* waiting room compare?

Do you feel at home, do you feel inspired by the surroundings and wish you could see more? Obviously it must be clean. Have the windows been washed since the doctor moved in? Do you intuit from any visual clues that you and this physician are striving in the same direction—or is his chosen atmosphere blasphemy in your book? For example, large stuffed animal heads protruding from the walls would indicate a radically different respect for mammalian life. And, as when entering a marriage, you need, at least, to feel jubilant in the early stages.

Finally, is it more like being in a hip hair salon, the lobby of a bus station, an experimental biosphere, or the White House Oval Office? I'd run screaming from the hair salon or the busy bus depot. The Oval Office might feel pretty good, as long as there were no gilded Louis XIV pieces looming at me to reinforce my lack of sophistication. Ostentatious evidence of the doctor's enormous wealth is probably a subtle strike against him.

This may sound odd, but if he's a little late, it probably means he's taking more time with his patients. Not such a bad thing. Plenty of doctors hustle through seven patients in an hour. Not bad in terms of turnover, but something makes me doubt these patients leave feeling satisfied. You can tell, in a consultation room, whether the doctor addresses you as a whole person or sees just the sag in your jowl.

A six-minute consultation is no consultation. Important to the assessment is the chemistry that develops between patient and doctor during the exchange.
—Dr. Stanley Klatsky

Peruse whatever reading material the doctor likes to share. One office was littered with stacks of brochures advocating "easy breast augmentation." Magazines must be scrutinized. What if you see the *Reader's Digest, Car and Driver,* and *Soldier of Fortune* on the table? Remember, every choice before you is either a statement or a lapse. Once, while waiting in a vet's office with a newborn goat in my lap, I overheard the doctor had taken the afternoon off to go deer hunting. This spoke volumes about our incompatibility, and I left. My new vet is more involved in saving critters than in recreational slaughter.

Who else is waiting with you? Are fishnet stockings and knee-high boots sitting to your left and right? Bingo, if that's your look. If not, don't get depressed. Plastic surgeons come in every style.

Are the walls covered in LeRoy Neiman paintings? Is the atmosphere formal, is it professional, or does it feel like day one at Club Med? Are strangers leaning together yakking to each other about what procedures they had last month? Would you like to join them or slide under the rug? Whatever whispers to you from the souls of your feet to the top of your head is a clue to where you should be.

Now for the surgeon's staff. Does the nurse chew gum and smoke? Speak English? Would her nail polish glow in the dark? He chose her to represent him and his practice, whatever she seems like to you. Would you say she's more like Anna Nicole Smith's twin or Diane Sawyer's sister? Do you feel comfortable around her? From where you sit, are you looking down your nose or up? Eye level would be best. Is she approachable? Once you're in the right office, it might be nice to establish a relationship with one nurse you can call with questions, most of which will be post-op.

All other things being equal, it's nice if you can work with a doctor whose taste matches your own. This way you'll be speaking the same language and using similar reference points, so neither of you will be the fish out of water. The guy who is perfect to work on Courtney Love may not be right for Candice Bergen. The guy who touches up Lena Horne might be out of the question for Snoop Doggy Dog.

Find someone you think you can trust and talk to. Fifty percent of plastic surgery is psychiatry, fifty percent is technical.
—Dr. Debra Johnson

I consulted with one doctor in the Southwest who had a great reputation among hairdressers (who are in a unique position to compare the quality of work done by local surgeons). But I couldn't get past his striking resemblance to Willie Nelson—long ponytail, same build, and the same vintage string tie. I had visions of leaving his operating room as a version of Wynonna Judd. Not so bad, frankly, but at the end of the day, not me. Another respected surgeon had photos of Wayne Newton in his waiting room, and wore more jewelry than I own altogether. His reputation was beyond reproach, but something just felt wrong.

My next waiting room had seventies' jungle wallpaper and lots of heavy geode ashtrays scattered around on tabletops next to the fake plants. You'd weep to know how many doctors I consulted, and how few I was comfortable with. Some acted like repressed Jesuits, disapproving of their profession and of me for being there. These were by far the most depressing. What if there's incense burning and a tarot reader practicing in the reception space? Unless your mother's a gypsy and your skirt is ruffled and red, simply pay up and leave. You're wasting everyone's time—most especially your own.

At last I found two or three offices that actually felt good. One was feminine (lovely wallpaper and trim) and very inviting, at least to my addled mind. The fresh-cut flowers were a calming touch, and the prints on all the walls made me imagine living there. It felt like an elegant women's club (probably too exclusive for me). Still, it was wonderful to be there, and soothing to consult with a woman (for once), though the rates were a little steep. I decided when my ship came in I'd visit her again. Then there was the Temple of Dendur waiting room, private, secure, and inspiring—possibly similar to the waiting room of the curator of the Louvre. The staff was extremely impressive, and I went back a time or two.

Architectural Digest would never photograph in the office I ended up liking best. Its armchairs, tables, and rugs were the jewels of a grandmother's attic, and subliminally I felt I was home. Everything was adequate (possibly even fine), but not a Ralph Lauren photo shoot. Since my life is not one either, it's not strange I felt relieved. The examining rooms were spotless and up-to-date. The doctor dressed as I hoped he might, and didn't want to sell me the Brooklyn Bridge. His lack of overstatement impressed me greatly, and his interest in anatomy was consistent with his choices of art in every room. This doctor was conservative in his approach and highly skeptical of many of the gimmicks that were the flavor of the month. He had dignity as well as humanity, and he seemed to possess far more wisdom than he needed to show and tell. At the right consultation I think, usually, you've got your answer before you're halfway through.

So, what if you don't feel great about anyone you've met? The whole endeavor should be a good experience, so research another town. Top doctors are scattered everywhere these days, and under no circumstances proceed with a conviction that's only lukewarm.

some personal tip-offs
for identifying dr. wrong

1. *Watch out for the guy who insists you need more extensive work than you had in mind to begin with. He may have a point, but take it slow.*
2. *Be alert to the stoic about pain medication. Maybe his mother was a Christian Scientist, but why should you have to suffer? (This won't be a laughing matter when you're hurting at 3 A.M.)*
3. *Beware of any doctor who you feel might shuffle you off to a colleague for the procedure once you're knocked out.*
4. *Be careful of the guy rushing you onto the table in forty-eight hours or less. One hopes he's in greater demand than that, but more*

importantly, I vehemently believe you need at least several weeks to prepare—practically, nutritionally, and emotionally.

The practical parts of preparing will be detailed next. Meanwhile, do two simple things to confirm you're off in the right direction. First, review the steps in your doctor research for any possible glitch—and remember, sleuthing could save the day, so make every inquiry you can. *Do not hesitate* to call the facility where your candidate has privileges to operate. If the place is tiny or unknown, let the warning bells sound. Second, remember that you may ask for the most recent reviews of his work, which are regularly assessed by his medical peers, who are keenly aware of his skills.

Beyond going to lengths like this, I have little more to say: Listen to your instincts, feet firmly on the ground, and imagine briefly the one your grandfather would choose, or at least the ones he'd rule out. Then go with your instinct and you'll come out looking great.

A good plastic surgeon can visualize in his mind the final result before he begins the procedure.

—Dr. Sherrell Aston

4

lamb to the slaughter:
plan and prepare

So you've found Dr. Right and you like him? Excellent.

The relationship established between you and your doctor is an integral part of your surgery and will become more intense as you progress through recovery. Ideally, you implicitly trust his judgment as an individual as well as his skills as a surgeon. It is important that he establish a professional tone and maintain it from beginning to end. After surgery, don't be surprised if his is the only opinion that matters to you. Everyone else will know nothing, and your doctor's daily pronouncements will take center stage in your mind.

You have, after all, entrusted him with your body and face to wound, heal, revitalize, and improve. His presence, his comments, and his phone calls will reassure you at pivotal moments when no one else can. He should be genuinely interested in the details of your condition and in your feelings as well. This is part of his job and he should take pride in doing it.

For six or eight weeks, you will be enveloped in an exclusive relationship with your surgeon. An imperceptible transference takes place then, during which you may come to trust and consult him as a father figure. It's equally possible you might develop a crush on him—or on his authoritative position in your life. Don't let this alarm you. It comes hand in hand with healing, and the subtle transference is a positive sign.

I have been privileged to conduct nearly one hundred interviews with plastic surgeons, anesthesiologists, dermatologists, and managing nurses. Plastic surgeons were by far the majority, and each of them was passionate about his work and gratified by each patient's success. The sincerity and thoroughness of your own doctor's concern should be impressive to you.

doctors' votes for famously bad lifts

Helen Gurley Brown	*Strom Thurmond*
Glenn Close	*Joe Pesci*
Glen Campbell	*Roy Scheider*
Carol Burnett	*Janet Leigh*
Michael Jackson	*Burt Reynolds*

so you think you might be ready?
start planning

You'll need a *minimum* of two weeks for the surgery and healing, so look deep into your calendar and find fourteen consecutive days that are absolutely free. Do it exactly as if you were planning a two-week trip to Europe or a rollicking Carnival Cruise. Organize everything so that your office, your clients, and the maintenance of your home will operate without your presence or your input. I can't stress how important this is.

Make arrangements to have some assistance for at least the first few days after surgery. If you decide to stay in a recovery facility, presumably it offers full-time care. Do inquire, however, as to whether it provides *round-the-clock* care for the first day or two.

Be sure that no friends expect to see you, and that daily stress can be kept to a minimum for at least the first ten days. You are likely to be in daily communication with your doctor or his office, even though you are supposedly unreachable by phone, so consider some method of screening your calls. And if you are inclined to get drop-in visitors, don't even think of answering the door.

You'll be in no position to drop your kids at school, settle an office dispute, clean out the hamster cage, or give instructions to the landscape crew. Your big job will be to:

• not talk (this includes smiling and laughing)
• keep your heartrate down

- follow orders regarding ice and application of cold packs
- keep your head elevated at all times
- sleep with your head propped up on three pillows for the first three to four days

Your doctor should give you a sheet of preoperative instructions. These will include a vast list of over-the-counter medicines, and certain vitamins and foods that must be eliminated from your repertoire. A good nutritionist will go several steps further, his or her goal being to prepare the body for the shock of surgery, to establish the best environment for healing, and to minimize side effects.

> *Aesthetic plastic surgery is an art form of the late twentieth century, and its practitioners are sculpting living human tissue. Unlike the great sculptors of the past, our medium is unforgiving and the result has to be perfect the first time.*
> —Dr. Sherrell Aston

You're ready emotionally if you've not only decided to do it, but on some subterranean level you're getting *excited* about the idea— the truest indicator of all that you're committed to make the leap.

One last time consider your motives, and how you expect the surgery to impact your life. Are you being realistic (and optimistic)—or do you secretly think your facelift will make all your dreams come true? Claudia Schiffer is a fluke of nature. No surgery produced her face. Please don't attempt to re-create yourself and emerge as someone new—it's emotionally unaffordable, financially insane, and it's not going to work. One woman in her late thirties is obsessed with making her face, body, and proportions exactly those of a Barbie doll. To date she has undergone twenty-six surgeries, and I doubt she's satisfied yet.

There are other aspects of surgery you should force yourself to confront. Occasionally (though rarely) a complication may develop and require an adjustment. Can you roll with this, trusting your doctor, or will you totally fall apart? The most common complication, a hematoma, is very easily treated and has no effect on your final result.

The ideal plastic surgery takes a physical problem and makes it a nonissue.

—Dr. Debra Johnson

A CEO I know was pretty good for two days after his lift. But by the third he was barking angry orders on the phone to his employees over an accounting error. His wife walked in and called 911 right away. She could see that his throat had ballooned (his internal stitches had burst with the strain) and he barely made it to the hospital in time. A maharaja's wife came to Boston for a facelift. Her surgery and recovery went so smoothly she decided to leave in five days, instead of waiting the recommended two weeks. Midway over the Atlantic she experienced severe hemorrhaging from the cabin pressure. Nothing like this should happen to you, since you know the consequences are real. But even if you're like General Schwarzkopf during the Persian Gulf War, you've got to kick back and relax.

the down and dirty

We are now approaching those crucial bits of information you're not necessarily eager to share with your doctor: menstrual period, hair coloring, chewing gum, eating, smoking, booze, excuses for why you're not at work, excuses for giving to friends, beauty maintenance (however minimal), good vitamins, bad vitamins, drug use (from Prozac to hard core), yeast infections, sex or no sex, hygiene, bedside necessities, antinausea tricks, etcetera. Let's start at the beginning, several weeks before your lift—ideally four to six, but you can make it on two.

giving your medical history means no omissions

The moment will roll around when the details of your medical history will be taken by the doctor, the anesthesiologist, or the nurse. The questions will range from medicines you currently take (or recently took), even over the counter, to family diseases (your aunt died on the table when her appendix was removed?), to allergies and tendencies toward excessive bruising or bleeding (even menstrual). Your doctor is not a narc, nor will anything you say shock him. Even in small towns, cosmetic surgery is being sought by dignified cross-dressers with genital warts, a history of chewing tobacco, and a lifelong battle with booze.

Let's start with booze, which includes NyQuil: You will have to be dry for two weeks before the surgery and another two weeks after. The big reason is you could unknowingly slip into post-op withdrawal, and who would know what to do? Also, the combination of alcohol and pain pills in just the right mix (sure, you know someone who got by with it once . . .) could mean the End of the Game. If this sounds extreme, run it by an anesthesiologist somewhere and see what he or she says. What about having your period? I have three answers: 1) A significant number of doctors do not like to operate during this time, on the theory there is excess bleeding; 2) most doctors say it's irrelevant; and 3) a few doctors are wary of the week prior to your period for smaller procedures, believing it to be a woman's most pain-sensitive week in the month.

regarding drugs

1. MARIJUANA. It's not as problematic as booze. Being deep into dope can present some of the same problems smokers have—pulmonary complications—but maybe not circulatory problems, which are nicotine's contribution. If for some idiotic reason you arrive at surgery stoned, *tell* them. The sedative as well as the amount of anesthesia will have to be readjusted, but that may be

the only consequence. The team in the surgery room is interested only in doing their job right, not in your personal habits—which means they need full disclosure from you.

2. COCAINE. Back in the eighties, people reportedly showed up for cosmetic surgery high on cocaine. Stupid ones anyway. The operation will be canceled the moment an arrhythmia (an irregularity in heartbeat) is detected. The extremely rare phenomenon of table death has been repeatedly traced to cocaine, which mingles in a most unfriendly way with the drugs that are necessary during surgery. I am told that using coke once or twice a week is far different from arriving high on surgery day. Daily use, however, emphatically increases your risk. Try not to be encouraged by this small distinction. We need to put the eighties behind us.

naturally aging beauties
or brilliant cosmetic work?

Sophia Loren	*Raquel Welch*
Diane Baker	*Phyllicia Rashad*
Elizabeth Hurley	*Jacqueline Bisset*
Candice Bergen	*Meg Ryan*
Heather Locklear	*Goldie Hawn*

3. BENZODIAZEPINES. The word sounds too exotic to be anything you're taking. But maybe Valium, Xanax, Librium, Dalmane, Restoril, and Klonopin don't. These and other benzodiazepines are not uncommon in many patient populations. Dr. Robert Schermer, an anesthesiologist and internist in Los Angeles, has

much to say on drug use relative to surgery. He urges his patients to come clean about absolutely everything—put everything on the table and let the medical team figure it out. Give your doctor a good strong history. Hold nothing back. It may save your life. Dr. Schermer swears he'd rather know of an honest addiction than cause a headliner death.

A few more tiny additions: MAO Inhibitors (monoamine oxidase inhibitors), often prescribed for depression, can have a significant effect on anesthesia. And certain rare eye drops for glaucoma must be discussed also. Having said all these ominous things, I frankly wasn't worried about this part at all. I was given something the doctor called "twilight sleep." The sleep part I can attest to, but the twilight part didn't lodge in my memory. Just try to remember through all the early details that in a couple of weeks you'll be ecstatic over the results (assuming you have no significant complications and your doctor does good work). Your role here is essentially a passive one. As Dr. George Semel stresses, "A successful surgery needs very little aftercare and a lot of preparation."

During the weeks prior to your surgery, maintain your fitness routine, eat sensibly, forget alcohol, and arrive rested. Don't go into surgery after a ten-day crash diet or an orgy. Enter the down time in good shape. You'll aim to resume your normal regimen gradually, within a few weeks, by listening to your doctor and your body.

pictures to remember you by

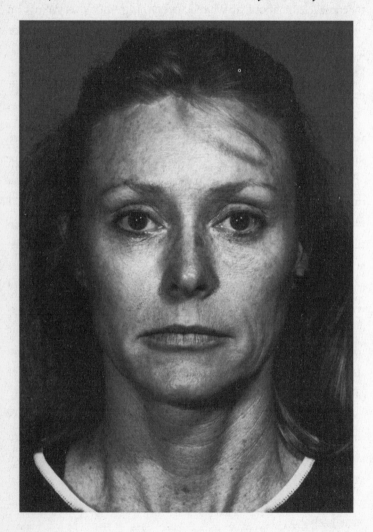

are excellent for future humility

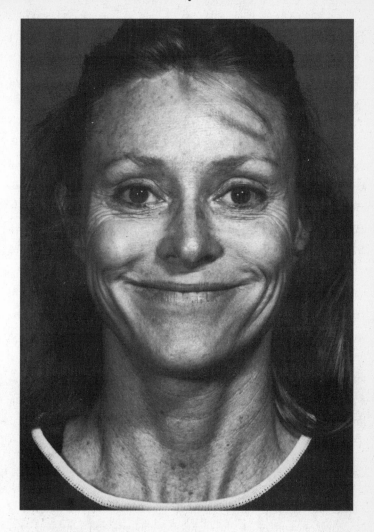

You will already have posed for the standard medical mug shots. These are generally hideous black and white shots of your face, taken from its worst possible angles and distorted into expressions you would normally try to conceal from the world at all times.

They will emphasize your flaws: slack wrinkled neck, bulging eyes, and the 2,000-wrinkle smile. (When any friend pulled out a camera, I used to reflexively suck my lower chin to the roof of my mouth to simulate a pastlife jawline. Pathetic. These tendencies will leave you after the lift.) The medical mug shots will be an invaluable road map for your doctor once you are in surgery. By the way, when it's all over, ask for your presurgery photos and keep them in a private place. Later, after a multitude of compliments, you may forget why you had the lift in the first place. The instant you start to think this way, dig out your mug shots from wherever they are and you will be justly humbled.

Two more things you might cover with your doctor beforehand: Would some decent pictures of yourself from five and ten years ago be helpful? He may say no, but if he wants them, be sure they're in his hands at least several days before surgery. Second, ask him if it would be helpful to show him pictures of features or looks you particularly dislike. Remember, you don't want to come out looking like a stranger. Reiterate your goals for improvement or restoration, and let the doctor do his job.

flash to all smokers

No surgeon will break into smiles when you tell him you currently smoke. Some doctors believe that if you smoked for twenty years and quit three years ago, the damage is done. The physical damage (as opposed to cosmetic) translates to poor circulation to your incisions, which greatly increases the odds for complications and bad scarring—not to mention the condition of your lungs. A lift could take anywhere from two to six hours, during which time you're under anesthesia and must be monitored and stable. With smokers, secretions are more likely to build up in the lungs, resulting in a productive cough and the possibility of post-op pneumonia. Dr. Robert Schermer feels that to eliminate breathing problems, you need to have quit smoking for four to six months prior to surgery—the longer the better. Furthermore, the nicotine patch may not be a great improvement over smoking. Though your lungs may have improved, your circulation will still be affected. Of the many doctors I spoke with, the most liberal on the issue of smoking said he would operate if the patient had quit entirely for one week before surgery and remained clean for two weeks after.

Here's the policy of Dr. Craig Foster in New York City, who led the surgical team that reconstructed the face of the Central Park Jogger. Dr. Foster will consider proceeding to surgery only if a smoker signs a separate Smoker's Consent Form stating she has been advised of the heightened dangers of smoking or being around smoke. If you're serious about getting a lift, decide on the moment for your last cigarette. Having plastic surgery and smoking butts are mutually exclusive concepts. Remember, you are wilting infinitesimally with every puff.

A woman is as old as she looks before breakfast.
—Edgar Watson Howe

to tell . . .

Though it might sound unimportant, begin to think about this: Are you going to announce roundly you're having a lift, or are you planning to be "away for a few weeks"? It has to be one or the other. Telling some and fudging to others will come to a crisis in no time, believe me. If you decide not to hide it, I understand. When it came down to the moment, I discovered it was impossible and unnecessary to lie in the face of someone I like. I personally feel enormously insulted when I am lied to and find it hard to get over. Added to which, I had no staunch reputation to protect as a neurosurgeon, feminist, or politician. Anyone who knew me would already realize I belong in the Silly Fringe Group—inclined to try cosmetic surgery and to know a good psychic in every town.

I do, however, have one suggestion that might prove useful: In your admirable candor, single out one or two appropriate friends from whom you will spare the truth. They will be your *control group*. Make it a point to see them a month after surgery, for lunch or dinner maybe. This will afford you an opportunity to watch their honest reactions, and thereby gauge the extent of your surgical success. Ideally, you want them to be thrown off balance, and to be inquisitive about how refreshed you look. Best of all—if they've known you for ten years, they might remember and recognize a former you. Needless to say, once you've determined you're glad you did it, the least you can do is provide the name of your doctor since they *are* your actual friends.

or not to tell . . .

It is infinitely more mysterious to obscure the fact of your surgery—that is to deny or lie, to shelter your glamorous persona. In this case, you must determine an airtight excuse to offer your friends, family, and co-workers. It needs to be consistent for all groups with the minuscule exception of your most trusted friend and/or housekeeper. For some women, taking this route is second nature and presents no problem whatsoever. (Think of the most frequently married and wealthy women you know.) My hat is off to them.

For others, strict guidelines must be established and observed. A quick selection of possible alibis: going to a spa, joining a Buddhist retreat group, helping out with a sick relative, visiting a terminal in-law, taking your godchild to Disney World, taking your own child to Disney World, attending a school reunion, going hiking in the Sierras, attending an open forum on the human genome project, or leaving town to meet a lover you'd prefer not to discuss just yet. You might, of course, come down with an illness or bug that drags on beyond two weeks, but this is dicey. Someone will impulsively stop in to bring you food or magazines. Concerned for your health, he or she will knock at every door and window, or wait until the doorman has you on the phone. The constant lying is debilitating, and it's difficult to convey illness in your voice day after day. One long good-bye in advance, with a tone that says, "I can't be reached," works best.

Let's pretend you chose the "fifteen days at a spa" line, and forge ahead. Tell people you're absolutely exhausted and plan to sleep the whole time—that you need to detach from the world and will certainly check in with the office. But you're not leaving a number, period. Plenty of people do it and so can you.

> *No woman should ever be quite accurate about her age. It looks so calculating.*
>
> —Oscar Wilde

One last thought: Once the physical healing is over and your lift "settles," you can take inventory much more objectively. There may be tiny changes (improvements) in your face that will be apparent to your more eagle-eyed acquaintances. Consider trying a new hair color, or cutting bangs, whatever's a departure from your norm. Although the eagle-eyed may notice a difference, they might attribute it to your new hairstyle. And vary your makeup a little. Brighten your lipstick color, darken your brows. Simple visual distractions should be adequate for the time being. Most people won't throw you up against a wall and demand an explanation. Do not, however, let your body weight fluctuate more than five pounds either way. Your cosmetic work was custom tailored for your body as it was.

now for the doctor's orders

Beware: You must avoid all aspirin products for two weeks before and after surgery.

These are ubiquitous and come under a hundred aliases. They can be either prescription or over-the-counter medications. And they contain either aspirin or ibuprofen. Check labels and if you're still unsure, ask your doctor or pharmacist. The reason is simple: Aspirin interferes with your blood's ability to clot. I once got a cut on my forehead, downed an aspirin for pain, and went to the Emergency Room—where it was hours before they were able to stop the bleeding and sew me up. I have a friend who chose to go to Venezuela for her facelift and nearly died on the table—due to a language problem regarding an over-the-counter aspirin-based product. Some approved over-the-counter substitutes are Datril, Fioricet, Panadol, and Tylenol.

Those that must be avoided:

Acetylsalicylic acid (aspirin)

Advil

Alka-Seltzer (pain reliever
    and/or antacid)

Anacin (any strength)

Anaprox

Anodynos DHC

Apa-San

Arthritis Pain Formula

Ascriptin

Aspergum

A.S.A. (aspirin)

Axotal

B-A-C, B-A-C with codeine

Bayer Aspirin (all types,
    maximum, children's
    and time released)

BC

Bexophene

Buffaprin

Bufferin

Buffets II

Buffex

Buffinol

Butalbital Compound

Cama arthritis pain reliever

Carisoprodol Compound

Cheracol Capsules

Clinoril

Codoxy

Cope

Coricidin

Damason-P

Darvon (with ASA or
    Compound)

Darvon-N (with ASA)

Diagesic

Dolene Compound

Doxaphene Compound

Dristan

Duradyne

Easprin

Ecotrin

Emcodeine

Empirin (also with codeine)

Equagesic

Equazine M

Excedrin

Feldene

Fiorgen PF

Fiorinal (also with codeine)

Gemnisyn

Isollyl Improved

Ibuprofen

Lanorinal

MAO Inhibitors

Magnaprin

Maprin

Marnal

Measurin

Meprogesic Q

Micrainin

Midol (caplets or for cramps)

Motrin

Naprosyn

Norgesic (also Forte)

Norwich aspirin

Nuprin

Percodan

Percodan-Demi

Presolin

Rid-A-Pain with codeine

Salatin

Saleto

Salocol

Sine-Aid

Sine-Off

Soma Compound (also with
    codeine)

St. Joseph aspirin for children

Stendil

Supec

Synalgos-DC

Talwin Compound

Triaminicin   Vanquish
Trigesic   Wesprin Buffered
Uracel   ZORprin

Eliminating the above products from your everyday regimen is a
basic presurgery requirement no one questions. Also, any hormones or hormone replacements you are taking should be discussed with your doctor and probably stopped. Hormones might
create bleeding and swelling during surgery, but this topic must
be decided between your gynecologist, your plastic surgeon, and
yourself.

   The following are California in origin. Feel free to laugh, but
just in case California doctors are on to something the rest of us
don't know about, avoid:

• anticholesterol drugs
• Benadryl
• lecithin
• large black Chinese mushrooms
• Chinese green tea and supposedly certain Chinese condiments

presumably because they, too, inhibit the body's ability to clot.

don't forget these

Take vitamin K for three to five days before surgery in five milligram tablets. Do not substitute another source of vitamin K. It is believed by many to greatly reduce the amount of bruising you will experience, and is prescribed by your doctor as Mephyton.

Some mainstream doctors suggest taking arnica (a homeopathic mountain herb), to minimize soreness as well as bruising, and bromelain (pineapple enzyme) to minimize inflammation of your incisions and even to aid digestion for two days before and after surgery. Many doctors don't include these in their instructions yet, but watch for this tendency to become more widespread in the future.

Again, many surgeons recommend that estrogen replacement therapy be suspended for two weeks before and two weeks after surgery.

If you have a heart murmur or any implants, facial or knee/hip replacements, speak with your doctor about starting antibiotics the day before your surgery rather than the day *of* surgery.

If you normally take vitamin E, stop two weeks beforehand. Apparently it has anticoagulant properties. Don't take any multivitamin that contains E, and if you happen to enjoy garlic tabs, do without them for a couple of weeks.

If you are a drinker, either stop drinking for two weeks before surgery or, at the very least, grind your alcohol intake down to one glass per day. Many doctors believe you should have no alcohol whatsoever for two or three days before. All of the above are conservative medical instructions.

If you prefer a homeopathic/nutritional approach, *here's a very condensed version from Dr. Elizabeth Dane, O.M.D., Ph.D., in Manhattan.*

SIX WEEKS PRIOR TO SURGERY AND FOUR WEEKS AFTER: Alcohol, cigarettes, all sugars, and coffee must be eliminated. They contribute to an acid condition in the body that impedes the healing process, may cause bleeding, and depletes the body's oxygen. More negatives are processed foods and white flour products, as well as dairy, which creates too much mucus and weakens the immune function.

Good things to ingest in their place:

Fiber—especially at breakfast, for flushing wastes and toxins.

Vegetables—carrots, parsnips, beets, sweet potatoes, asparagus, dark leafy green veggies. Skip regular potatoes (it's a long story).

Fruits—papaya, grapefruit, strawberries, and green seedless grapes.

Herbal teas—burdock root, juniper berries, and horsetail grass flush the kidneys; dandelion root, Angelica, *and bayberry support the liver; goldenseal, echinacea, and* Astragalus *fight infection; red clover tops and alfalfa leaf clean the blood.*

Cranberry juice—flushes both stagnant water and lymphatic fluids common after surgery. Must use the health-food concentrate rather than the grocery-shelf kind.

TWO WEEKS BEFORE: Take arginine and ornithine, to add white blood cells; chelated iron to strengthen cells and eliminate bleeding; B_{12} and folic acid to speed up healing.

Increase: *lysine, amino acid tablets, antioxidant tablets, acidophi-*

lus and chlorophyll, calcium and magnesium, B-complex, vitamin C and bioflavonoids, and alfalfa tabs.

Stop completely: *vitamin E and selenium.*

THREE DAYS BEFORE AND AFTER: take Bromezyme (by Karuna), one or two tablets three times per day, to stop bruising.

TWO DAYS BEFORE AND AFTER: Take arnica, four tablets, three times per day.

SURGERY DAY: Take arnica, four tablets, three times per day; vitamin C, one tablet every two hours; and bioflavonoid, one tablet every two hours.

All of the above are based on Dr. Dane's years of experience with both women and men who have successfully undergone facelift surgery.

some personal information

You will need help around the clock from the moment you wake up for the next two or three days. These arrangements must be firmly in place before you enter surgery. The question is whether or not you need to spend the first night or two in a hospital setting. Your doctor's opinion will be the deciding factor. Often, for a pure facelift, you may be allowed to leave (with assistance) at the end of the day. For convenience, you might choose to stay in the hospital with a private nurse for a day or more. Also, if you've had a number of things done (say, lipo on the thighs, a tummy tuck, a facelift, and eyes), do let me suggest that you stay in the hospital, where you can be carefully monitored.

One little extra I strongly recommend is hiring a private nurse to be at your side for at least the first twenty-four hours. Hospitals are nice, but you can die waiting for the nurse you buzzed to finally get to your room. Generally, a hospital's floor nurses are overloaded. What you need is someone glued to your bedside who can minister to you constantly. For all practical purposes, you might as well be under anesthesia the first twenty-four hours or more.

Possibly the private nurse (your doctor's office can provide recommendations), as well as a friend can help you get home and settled into your bed, propped up. Here's what it translates to:

Someone beside yourself will have to bring fresh cold ice packs to hold softly around your temples, jaws, and eyes as frequently as every fifteen minutes, at the outside every thirty. The one person who won't be up to the job is you, no matter how hardy you think you are. You need to be resting mindlessly in a propped-up position, slipping in and out of consciousness while (just this once) someone else does the work.

Do not even contemplate attacking the ice trays. This treatment during the first twenty-four hours (at least) is extremely relevant to the quality of your long-term healing. Don't drop the ball here. Either stay overnight in a hospital that provides this service, or hire a private nurse to come home with you for one or two days. She's a pro, she'll dress your wounds, and she'll give you the prescribed medicines at the right intervals—even if she has to wake you gently to do it.

coloring your hair?

In the likely event that you apply color to your hair (tints, single process, highlights, or rinse), get out your datebook. Hair coloring and perms are ruled out for four to six weeks post-op. So color your hair several days before the big event—which means not on the morning of or even the day before. Three or four days in advance is fine. Later, when you emerge from your cocoon, liberated and delirious with joy, there will be no telltale roots skulking around to bring you down. Do not—even in the spirit of change—let yourself be persuaded to try an extreme cut (or buzz cut) right now. You'll be counting on the hair you've got to cover your scars.

A few other items you'll want to have on hand are a *hair dryer with a setting for cool or very low;* some baby shampoo and later some No More Tangles rinse, both by Johnson and Johnson. You will be treating your hair—and your head—with extreme delicacy for several weeks. No hot rollers; no massaging the scalp in a lather; no vigorous brushing; no mousse, hairspray, or other high-tech products. Just limp clean hair. You won't mind, believe me.

pills and prescriptions

While we're on post-op trivia, discuss with your doctor before surgery which pain pills work best for you. (Do some make you nauseous? Is codeine a good choice? If one doesn't feel right, can he predetermine a substitute?) Sleeping pills are another consideration. You may need them to reestablish your sleep patterns, so work out in advance what's best for your system. You can easily leave these minutiae to your doctor and to fate, but it will simplify life if you fill the prescriptions beforehand. Leaving this undone until after surgery means someone will have to scramble to fill them for you when you're released from the hospital. You will not be up to stopping by the pharmacy on the way home. After the surgery you'll be in one piece, but not mobile or very alert. And nowhere near as resourceful as you normally are.

stock up

Let's talk about your first meal after surgery, or semi-meal as the case may be. Florida's Dr. Roxanne Guy is an expert on women's recovery. She recommends that when you resume eating, you do it very, very slowly. Start with a few sips of water. If that goes down easily, later move on to a soft drink or tea. No rushing and gulping even if you're starved. Give it some time. Your next step may be some crackers that will dissolve in your mouth and won't require you to chew. Take these steps slowly. The actual day of surgery, you'll probably stick with small amounts of liquids.

As you return to normal eating, consider soup or mashed potatoes. Your digestive system will be in a delicate condition, so don't push it. Soft and bland are the words to remember. Don't even think about anything spicy or the least bit hard to chew. You've got the rest of your life for that. Avoid chewing for now.

Good prospects for your fridge are healthy soups; pureed vegetables; applesauce; oatmeal; cottage cheese; pureed anything provided it's bland; and low-fat yogurt. Frozen is nice, but if you're inclined toward yeast infections, remember that you may be on antibiotics, so an active culture would be best to replace the good bacteria. Not many frozen yogurts contain active cultures, but the few that do say so on the container.

Some other foods that can help with your recovery are: freshly prepared fruit juices; bananas; smooth peanut butter; broth and saltines; tofu; pureed broccoli soup with chicken broth and half and half; blender combinations of fruit, milk, yogurt, honey, and so on; nonchewy soups; baby food (some love it . . .); milk shakes; MetRex protein drinks; and plain rice cooked in broth.

One head nurse stressed that protein expedites healing. Ask *your* doctor about healing foods, but remember, nothing chewy or spicy.

the facelift bedside survival kit

I consider the following items to be absolute essentials for a fully comfortable recovery. I wish like hell I'd had these things on my bedside table. I didn't, though some of them finally trickled in. If any of the following seem extreme to you, circle them and look at them again when you're a day or two into recovery.

1. A box of *flexible straws,* so you can receive nutrition without having to chew, at least for a few days.

2. *Plaque-loosening mouthwash.* Your teeth might feel dirty, but the pain of introducing a toothbrush might bring you to your knees. Keep the straws and mouthwash together. Even if you can't open wide and brush hard, your mouth will feel tidier.

3. *Q-Tips* to help you clean your incisions over the coming weeks.

4. *Hydrogen peroxide.* A large bottle will be very welcome. This too may be handy for rinsing your incisions.

5. *Antinausea suppositories,* if you're the queasy type. Between anaesthesia and pain pills, your stomach might revolt. They absorb quickly and last a long time.

6. *A slender, child-size toothbrush or an eyebrow brush* for when you do start brushing your teeth. Until then, glycerin-coated Q-Tips may work nicely, or at least rinsing with warm salt water.

7. *Gauze pads* for dressing and tidying your wounds.

8. An oversized dropper (for dispensing liquid medicine to infants). All drugstores carry them. Helps to remove the peroxide deftly from its container and aim it right at your incisions when you rinse. Pouring directly from the peroxide bottle is a disaster.

9. *Refillable Ziploc plastic bags* to hold ice chips and water. Rather than being balloon tight, they feel best if they softly conform to your face (or other surgical site). Some doctors and nurses advocate buying five or six bags of frozen peas for this purpose. Whichever you choose, they must be rotated frequently from the freezer so the chilled part touching your face is always extremely cold.

10. *Gyne-Lotrimin,* if you're inclined toward yeast infections, which might result from taking antibiotics.

11. *Milk of magnesia* (or another mild laxative). Pain pills often contribute to constipation. You'll know if you're the type.

12. *Abundant sturdy pillows* to help you sleep propped up. A foam wedge at the bottom might not be a bad idea.

13. *A pharmacy that delivers* would be awfully nice. Maybe you can establish this in advance.

14. *A true friend* who's available to drop in a lot the first few days, as well as to phone to see what you need. She is the person you can complain to. She'll remind you why you did this in the first place.

15. *A supply of videos* you may want to watch, though probably not for the first day or two.

16. *Some books on tape* you never got to read. If they're good for anything, this is it. Should you be up for it, you can also attempt to learn a new language on tape.

17. Ask Dr. Right whether you'll need bacitracin, Cortaid, or another *antibacterial lubricating ointment.* If the answer is yes, ask him if he'll send you home with it, or whether you should add it to your list of supplies to be purchased in advance.

18. *If you have a speakerphone* and have never used it, figure out how. For the first few days you will *not* want to hold a receiver to your ear. It's manageable, but . . .

19. This last is for the very tender-eared people of the world. The *special pillow* I created under duress has been treasured by many, and most people won't give them back. After you have been sitting propped up for several days or lying on your back,

you may be eager to roll onto your side, especially if you have back problems. The pillow is earless, and lets your spine continue in a straight line when you are on your side, rather than crooking your neck up or letting it droop. It is only to be used when you no longer need to elevate your head for sleeping. More on this in the following chapter.

now you can relax because . . .

You have prefilled all prescriptions you will need after your surgery.

You have asked your doctor's office if you need to bring any prescriptions to the hospital with you.

You have decided whether to stay in the hospital overnight (or longer), or whether you would prefer to go home accompanied by a private nurse. Even if you stay in the hospital overnight, you will have remembered to hire a private nurse.

Some people, I must warn you, report a reactionary depression in the aftermath of surgery. It's possible I experienced it, but I was too busy adjusting to the limitations that follow surgery to notice. I was woozy from the anesthesia and sleeping a lot. Then I was trying to feel with my fingers what had been done and where. What do people expect after major surgery . . . elation? For me, the low point was suddenly fearing I'd made a horrible mistake. This moment of panic gripped me on the day after surgery, probably the most uncomfortable day of all, when I saw my swollen face (monstrous) and fully realized I was incapacitated. Recovery was impossible to imagine on that first post-op day. By day two I was better and the fear had left. Pain pills were my crutch. I had never envisioned recovery as a time for celebration or receiving guests. It's about keeping still and healing and paying attention to your body. Know what to plan for and it's less likely you'll be depressed.

sleep well

After your last supper, get to bed on time. No liquids, no gum chewing, not even Alka-Seltzer. You might want to set two alarm clocks. Don't sleep through it after getting this far.

> *I'm tired of all this nonsense about beauty being only skin deep.*
> *That's deep enough. What do you want—*
> *an adorable pancreas?*
>
> —Jean Kerr

5
surgery day
. . . *and after*

*One doesn't discover new lands without consenting to lose
sight of the shore for a very long time.*

—André Gide

*b*efore you even open your eyes you realize this is the day. Be
calm and methodical. Don't brush your teeth (you might
swallow some water), and skip coffee and breakfast. Feed
the cat and water the plants. Put the tape on your answering
machine that says you're away for two weeks.

You'll be a new person when you return.

Don't leave home without:

- an oversized scarf to come home in (and not your finest one;
  leave the Hermès at home. . . .)
- sunglasses to hide behind
- comfortable, steady, flat shoes you do not have to lace up
- clothing you can put on and peel off easily without touching

your head, such as a dress or top that buttons down the front or back

- your checkbook (you will probably need to write a check to pay your nurse[s]. If you particularly liked her, add a 10 percent tip.)
- a credit card—you shouldn't really need it, but if some charge has been overlooked and you don't have a way to pay it, you'll be sorry.

Do not *take to the hospital:*

- any jewelry
- any furs
- any makeup applied to your face
- any fabric containing nylon, such as knee-high socks or stockings (these interfere with electrodes)
- a nightgown or bathrobe—you will have to wear the hospital gear anyway, and you will not be socializing
- painted fingernails or toenails, since the exact color of your skin must show through at all times.

You have established that your doctor and his medical team are an extremely competent group. *You did not lapse into the laziness of wishful thinking instead of doing your research on this subject.*

You've checked out your doctor from several points of view, and with luck, have spoken to patients whose opinion you trust. Everything is preorganized for the time you will return.

Be on time when you check in for surgery, which means,

frankly, be early for once. Don't tamper with the delicate chore-ography of your surgeon's schedule. Though it's hard to believe, his is more critical than your own.

Stay calm and stalwart this morning. Pray to your God and make resolutions. Any conflicts you might suddenly have about proceding should not be worn on your sleeve. Whining to the nurses and other workers around you, at this point, will endear you to no one. It would be nice to have a friend deliver you to the hospital, but when you'll really need her is afterward—to assure you it's finally over, and remind you whose idea it was from the start. More important, line her up to whisk you delicately from the facility back to your home. You will not be marching down halls or blowing kisses from the back of the car. Crouched be-neath your oversized scarf, you'll be muttering prayers that the roadway is smooth. A steady arm to guide you to bed is exactly what you'll need. This arm should belong to a friend you trust to see you at your rock-bottom, disoriented, bandaged worst. If no one in your life qualifies, you may want to forget the lift and find someone.

In my life, there was only one person who could orchestrate this like a pro. I recruited her help to rudder me through it weeks before I even began to shop for a doctor. Appoint this person to handle anything unexpected that may come up, since you won't have much perspective for a couple of days. She needs to be familiar enough with your life to know you as a sister would. You will either spend surgery night in the hospital or return to your home with a nurse. Your friend doesn't have to sleep over, but dropping in (at least) once a day would be good. And, naturally, if her heart's in the right place, she'll call on a regular basis to see how you feel and what you need.

your nurse

You must have a nurse full time at your bedside for the first twenty-four hours post-surgery, whether you're in the hospital or in your home. Her job is not a small one and should *greatly affect your results.*

Your nurse will administer the proper medicines at the proper intervals, and ceaselessly refresh (no naps) your cold packs throughout the first night. Also, your nurse is trained to watch for signs of a problem—so don't think you'll economize by replacing her with a novice or a pal. Inquire in advance what you'll owe her for each twelve-hour shift, and keep your checkbook near your bed. If you decide you need her longer, arrange that as soon as you can. And if she was especially heroic or noble, remember to tip her well. If you have any, give her some flowers.

one doctor's letter to facelift patients

Dear Patient,

You have just had an extensive operation on your face and this letter may help you through the next few days. It is not a substitute for personal attention, and your doctor should see you during each office visit. It is merely the answers to many questions that you may have. These answers are now before you, and you can refer to them at your leisure. During the operation, the skin of your temples, cheek, and neck have been freed widely from your facial muscles and all possible excess has been trimmed off and thrown in the waste bucket. It can not come back.

Your tissues resent this "turning the clock back" and will react with swelling and a feeling of tightness, which will be reponsible for some discomfort but very little actual pain. The incisions were closed with tension and will be tender for a time. The undercutting and the pull to lift the face occasionally is responsible for some numbness to the cheek areas. Rarely, an ear may be numb, but all areas usually regain their sensation eventually.

After the operation, a pressure dressing is placed about the face and neck to help hold the tissues in their new position until they have had a chance to become fixed. This pressure also discourages bleeding. A sudden swelling of the cheek with a shutting eyelid and a feeling of severe tenderness suggests there is some bleeding under the skin. This clot is not a danger to you, but for more rapid healing is better removed early. Your nurse will contact the doctor if she feels it is necessary. Your recovery will still be quite normal except for a little more black and blue discoloration. This will subside in a few weeks, but its absorption can be speeded by warm compresses after the second week. Take care not to have these too hot! Test on the back of your hand, as your face may be numb. Of necessity and in an attempt to get the best possible result, all wounds have been closed under tension. You are warned not to twist your head or otherwise stretch your neck for the first four days. When looking to the side, turn the body with the head, keeping the neck quiet. Moderation in stretching and twisting is advised for one month.

Your bandage will be changed once before you go home. This is usually done the day after the operation. Most patients are discharged on the second morning after surgery, particularly if they have someone to help them at home. Leaving the hospital with a head bandage makes it wise to have a large scarf with you to wrap over your dressing. Call your doctor's office for an appointment on the third or fourth day after surgery. At this visit, your dressing will be changed, some of the stitches will be removed, and a light dressing applied.

All stitches will have been removed by the seventh day and from then on no dressing is necessary. Eyebrow plucking and makeup are now permissible. A shampoo and hair setting can be carried out on the eighth day. Tinting and dyeing is allowed after the tenth day. [Other doctors recommend waiting longer.] Use a hairstylist who is familiar with this operation. If you do not have a favorite, ask the nurse or your doctor's office for suggestions.

Your cheek areas will show early swelling and possibly a slight discoloration. Due to gravity, this will settle in the neck on its way out. You will probably be presentable to the public ten days after surgery and certainly in two to three weeks. How quickly you get rid of the swelling and discoloration depends on your health and healing quality as well as a quiet, careful, calm convalesence.

A facelift will naturally be stretched by the early swelling, and when this subsides, a little of the gain is lost. This gives a natural effect and prevents the drawn, masklike appearance. Many ask if their face will fall or if they will be worse when it does. No, it will not fall and no, it will not be worse. Your excess sag and droop have been removed and thrown away so they cannot come back. Your skin tone has improved and you will always be a step younger than your years. However, your skin is naturally going to age again. If, after several years, your skin has aged more than pleases you, a second facelift at a slightly reduced fee may be advisable, and this should then carry you ten years or more.

To safeguard the result you have gained, you are urged to avoid excessive gain and loss of weight. The stretch and slack will play havoc with your work. Do not allow severe facial massage. Moderate sunshine if enjoyed is permissible. Too much sun will dry and tan the skin to leather and increase the wrinkles many-fold.

It is not the lot of everyone to grow old gracefully and thus plastic surgery has been perfected so that people can continue to be attractive to themselves and their friends. It is important to keep a good-looking person attractive while still young enough to enjoy it. The average age for a facelift is in the middle fifties, but a healthy seventy-five also deserves a new lease. The operation merely removes excess skin, which is no different from ridding the body of other unnecessary and undesirable appendages, such as appendix or tonsils. There is no need for a feeling of guilt nor is there reason for broadcasting. Let everyone enjoy your new attractiveness, and if someone should guess the secret, do not be upset.

Good luck and good health,
>Malcolm A. Lesavoy
>Professor, Division of Plastic and Reconstructive Surgery, UCLA
>Chief of Plastic and Reconstructive Surgery, Harbor/UCLA, Torrance, California

closer and closer: preregistration

A couple of days before surgery, I preregister on a stinking hot day. I am attached to various machines and inspected inside and out, while contemplating my utter insignificance in our monstrous universe—a topic that's stuck with me for weeks. Though in terms of genuine risk a facelift is probably the tonsillectomy of adulthood, the anesthesia part worries me. It's simply not possible that good female maintenance now involves risking my life. *All Mama used was Nivea oil and the rare lick-and-stick-on Frownie. I face two hours of unconscious bone-level cleanup to be revalued by those I know best.* But this is progress.

"Allergic to any medications?" and "Excuse me, but what is your age?" are the only words I hear. A reference to "helmet dressing" calls to mind the chef salad I won't be eating for weeks.

I'm hoping a side effect might be weight loss, the silver lining in most women's clouds. Hawthorne's definition of sin is abandoning your heart for your head. This often reaffirms me, but not today.

the "ostrich" approach

I decide to take a sanitized view and not contemplate the physical facts of surgery. That is, I bury my head in the sand. This behavior explains why, if complications arise, we often feel we were never warned. I deafen myself to the downside, envisioning a facelift to be only slightly worse than the wisdom-tooth ordeal. The more rational approach would be to thoroughly absorb the range of risks and potential discomforts involved. If the benefits greatly outweigh the risks (and they should), that's your informed green light. I leap in with blind trust in my surgeon and very little actual education—and in retrospect I think I was wrong. Had we hit the odd snag, instead of being aware of possible complications and how they could be solved, I might have needlessly panicked—and left my doctor to keep a level head for both of us, which would have been unfair.

nurse peggy

Irish Peggy Broderick is redheaded and attractive, one of the best-known figures on New York's plastic surgery beat. She is and has been for fifteen years, managing nurse in New York City's (and the world's) busiest facility for cosmetic work. Peggy has seen thousands of facelifts and personally tends to recovering patients at the designated intervals. She has provided encouragement and direction for many young physicians. And she is an extraordinarily wise woman with a rare knack for boiling utter chaos down to bare facts in the blink of an eye.

   A few bits of Nurse Peggy's wisdom:

- *A facelift is just a skin and muscle operation, not invasive. It's not heart or brain surgery or work on an organ.*
- *It's unfortunate that patients go through such agonies of anxiety before surgery.*
- *Many doctors play their own favorite music in the O.R., from country western to Beethoven.*
- *Most people don't want to know the surgical details.*
- *A hematoma? (Her eyes roll.) It needs to be drained. It's more of a nuisance than a risk to the final result.*
- *A sedative en route to surgery helps. The patient is ready to donate her body to science by the time she gets to the O.R.*
- *A patient lingers in recovery for two to five hours, until nausea looks unlikely and blood pressure returns to normal.*
- *When the blood pressure is normal, the patient begins to ooze. This is a good sign.*
- *When a patient twists around in the first twenty-four hours is when a hematoma occurs.*
- *Take it easy when you leave the hospital. You'll look your worst forty-eight hours after.*
- *Expect your face to be lopsided in swelling, bruising, and healing. One side always takes the brunt. Often nurses observe it to be the left side. We don't know why.*

- *There are limits to what you can do with human tissue and what a surgeon can do.*
- *Never lie about* any *preexisting conditions, such as asthma, heart problems, vascular problems, use of anticoagulants, etcetera. The lie can cost you your life.*
- *The only thing any patient needs to know is that she's in the hands of a very competent surgeon she can trust.*

the night before surgery

By now numb, I'm assured by pros this will stop my age clock for eight years. I feel meek and still and tiny and my heart must be having a nap. I recognize this as my mode for conserving strength when something serious looms ahead. So I write a nervous letter to my daughter (nine months old) at midnight, discouraging her from feeling she might ever need cosmetic help: *Dear Miss Pie . . .*

5 A.M. my surgery day

The alarm dings in the dark, so I dress for my hospital date—in a loose-fitting dress that can be folded around me. I decide a short predawn walk to the hospital will be my gesture to fitness for the coming month. During these brisk fifteen minutes, I see barely five moving cars. Inexplicably, the tape in my mind singsongs "Three Blind Mice" over and over. When lyrics relentlessly lock into my brain, I've recently figured out, it's a message from the inner me to examine the words. In this case I refuse and revert to a conversation from the previous night that managed to cheer me up. It was a beau from my early twenties registering his vote against my lift. I will love him always for thinking I don't need it.

I arrive at the hospital, am told where to go, and mentally shrink into a bird. The large waiting area could easily be a bus station. I create a small back-story explaining what brought each person to this place. I'm surprised to envy the ones with someone holding their hand. I chose this date carefully to coincide with my husband's absence from town. I thought I didn't want him to see me ooze and swell and groan and slowly heal. Now I do. But he's asleep on another coast as I approach the guillotine. My doctor pages me in the bus station, and I am directed to a phone. He sounds incredibly alert. He is reassuring and says I'll do great. I take this to heart as absolute fact and instruct all my cells to do so as well.

God, it's hell being lucid at 5 A.M.!

I am shown to a locker for my clothes. Metal lockers remind me too much of school, so I pretend they are wood. I am provided with paper surgery clothes, and shuffle to another holding room. Looking up from my gurney, I see that I'm rolling down narrow, well-trafficked halls. The hospital seems like a massive anthill housing extremely busy ants. Finally I spot my doctor as he arrives covered in paper clothing from his hairnet to his feet. I am the cliché patient in that I have absolute trust in this man. He squeezes my hand paternally as my anesthesiologist appears. I'm amazed that no one looks sleepy. All corners of the room turn

black as I contemplate in a woozy fashion whether my anesthesiologist is in fact a television actor on the side . . .

recovery:
a mini-preview

*Along with the possibility of discomfort, the anesthesia will leave you
exhausted and possibly disoriented for the first few days. I constantly
took naps, woke up shortly, and thought twenty-four hours had
passed. For whatever reason, feelings of physical fragility dominated
my every thought and every contemplated motion. I was consciously
grateful not to have earthquakes to worry about.*

*I don't mean to paint a grim picture of early recovery—surpris-
ingly there are many passive things you can enjoy, though not the
ones I had planned. A few are music, heavenly naps, books on tape,
and extremely abbreviated visits from friends (three to five minutes), if
they annoyingly insist. I liken these mini-visits to cars slowing down
on the freeway to get a cheap peak at an accident. Pretending you're
out of town may be your best protection, provided you have a pharmacy that delivers and either a housekeeper or devoted friend to make
sure you're comfortable.*

*The likelihood of a significant complication is very low—but your
doctor is only a phone call away. It's better to be a minor telephone
pest than to suffer a crisis in silence. Here are a few symptoms to
watch for:*

• *excessive tenderness and swelling of a particular area in your face or
  neck*

- *persistent vomiting (more than the isolated incidence of vomiting that may be a temporary reaction to pain medication or anesthesia).*
- *fever.*

The time for healing is good time for reflection, and you'll be absorbed in watching the physical changes day by day. I thought I could update my address book, answer some letters, and catch up on several books. It didn't turn out that way for me, but it easily could for you. Because I need glasses to read, I had two problems.

Since I lacked sufficient earlobe to hide the facelift scars, my doctor had to somehow extend my earlobes in order to do the job. (I dare not contemplate what this entailed, but my ears fit entirely differently against a telephone receiver now.) I wasn't eager to hang glasses over them, and because my upper lids were tucked, my vision was blurred by medicinal ointment for at least a couple of days. If you need reading glasses and find they don't attach so well, consider holding them in front of your eyes with a giant clothespin or its equivalent—like a lorgnette. Since my lift, I've determined the limits of what can and cannot be accomplished in those first few days. Remember, I had no one to ask.

Happily you're not in that position.

immediately post-op

I am nestled warmly in a slow-moving glacier, hearing strange and familiar things. The glacier halts and a blinding light splashes into my face, then somebody sounds like my friend Sooz. My first sight is her damn flashbulb, since to be evil, she is documenting this. Still, I'm extremely glad she's with me in this cheerful room I've never seen before. It's odd waking up in a place that's not where I went to sleep. Without moving, I know I've been injured, though I sense it's under control. Everything relative to my head is tender and I know better than to try to move. It isn't pain really, but I strongly suspect pain lurks just a few steps away.

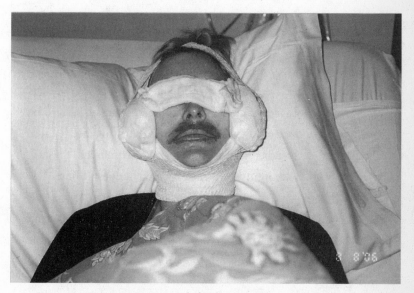

post-surgery, pre-consciousness, and clearly irresistible.

A fuzzy Sooz steps in front of my bed and I remember where I am, and why. Swimming back into consciousness takes longer than it should. Meanwhile, my will is clenching its teeth to escape where I am and go home—but I haven't the tiniest drop of strength for this, and I drift out to sea again. Because I can swallow, I realize there have been no tubes in my throat and thank God I wasn't left partially awake. My doctor pops in with the sickening report that one eyelid contained some extra fat and one side of my face took more time. I later correlate this information with the side that took longer to heal.

God knows why this is the criterion, but my doctor refuses to release me from the hospital to go home until I triumphantly pee.

night on the day of my surgery

With the assistance of Sooz as well as a nurse, I am carefully shepherded home. Reentering my building is a total blur. I was supported on both sides and afraid to walk. And embarassed to be seen by my doorman. Since I was afraid to turn my head, I still don't know if Freddie dropped his jaw or continued to look straight ahead. Back in my own bed, it actually doesn't hurt. Yes, there is stinging and swelling, but nothing compared to a mean case of cramps. Being unable to move my head is unsettling and makes me nervous. It is tightly bandaged to hold unthinkable things in place. I wish I'd seen a video showing me the various post-op stages.

Then again, I didn't want to know.

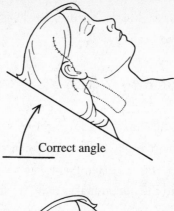

Correct angle

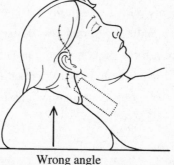

Wrong angle

It's important to sleep practically sitting up—to keep my chin raised instead of drooped onto my chest. The drooped position cuts circulation to the areas where it's needed and precipitates disaster. But sleep is the wrong word for what occurs on surgery night. Intermittent dozing is more like it. I've fallen asleep twenty times, but my nurse, doing her job, keeps replacing my ice packs, giving me on average fifteen minutes of sleep at a time. Annoying as hell, but bless her, I'm too tired to be doing it myself and I know it's crucial to healing well.

the day after surgery

I am a mass of mutilation stacked upright in bed. This occurs to me when I am almost awake. At least it's the morning *after*. Still, I am helpless and feeling not great. I envision navigating from here to the kitchen, and the notion makes me want to faint. At fifteen minute intervals, my nurse robotically changes the icy things molded onto my temples, eyes, and jaw. These areas were constantly chilled through the night and are for half of the following day. The general discomfort and exhaustion left me little appetite, though I did sip clear soup from a straw and let saltines melt in my mouth.

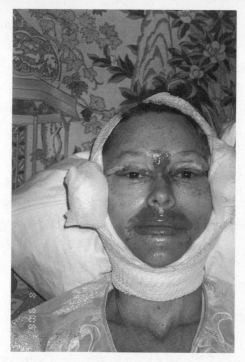

A natural gift for swelling. You will never feel uglier than this.

day one . . . still

Am surprised by how small and vulnerable I feel and how fearful of motion I am. My fingers have discovered translucent drainage tubes running out of the back of my neck. They circle forward to meet in a clear plastic bulb, creating a dripping red necklace of blood. I must have felt great for a while, since the bloody gro-tesqueness inspired me to pick up the phone and invite my finicky neighbor by. In a gentlemanly way, he complied and dropped in—to be immediately overcome with revulsion while retaining his formal veneer. Like Fred Astaire dropping in on his sister and finding a monster in her bed. He emitted a violent squeal with a question mark on the end. Shortly after this moment of glory, the pain pill began to fade. I prayed for no earthquakes and a decent chunk of sleep.

You will not be able to swivel your head to look from right to left. You will have to enlist your whole upper body and turn it slowly from the waist, without changing the position of your head relative to your neck.

day one drags on

For me, the worst. My face is the size of a pumpkin and growing. For several hours I have panicky thoughts of bad judgment and regret. I have to strain to remember what drove me to this.

If you begin to question your judgment, I know what you need. Ask your doctor for some Xeroxes of your worst "Photos from Before." Had these been at my bedside, they would have sobered me up in a snap. But they weren't, and a tiny cloudfront moved into my bedroom and rained on me most of the day. Looking this bad makes it impossible to imagine looking different.

I believe my surgeon is the busiest man on earth. He is, for example, booked solid until a date fifteen months from today. The

President has it easy compared to him. Although still no one believes me, this man was able to squeeze in a house call, for which *I am indebted to him for life*. (Though his office is not far away, on that very first day following my facelift, I'm not sure I could have made it there.) He removed my helmet and dressings (the source of discomfort from pressure) and examined my face in the light. (Had I stayed overnight in the hospital, these would have been removed the morning after as a matter of course.) Before vanishing, my doctor pronounced I was healing well. Just that one day, I felt physically helpless and was spiraling into despair. His visit and inspection turned everything around. My gratitude for the kindness of his gesture can never be fully expressed. I plan to do small things for each of his children for the next thirty years of my life.

I now know many women who had facelifts and never experienced pain. The discomfort is unquantifiable, and differs from case to case. Each human handles pain differently, and your attitude can help a lot. I was certainly no stoic about pain medication. The best one for me was Vicodin, which also helped me sleep. Food was interesting in concept only, and I yearned to brush my teeth. But parting my teeth half an inch was a paralyzing thought. What tided me over was placing a flexible straw into some festive mouthwash for fighting plaque. I could suck, savor, slosh, and eject it. This idiotic ritual braced me with confidence that I would soon be able to take care of myself again.

I check my watch repeatedly and am shocked how the hands barely move. I keep hoping to wake from each nod-out four hours later, but when I wake up, it's usually five minutes from the last time I looked. After my longest nap, I woke up certain a whole day had passed, when it had been only half an hour.

Unquestionably the day after surgery was the longest day of the year. But it fades to nothing in your memory. And the results are emphatically worth it, although on this day you may look like a wreck.

It is amazing how complete is the delusion of beauty.
—Leo Tolstoy

In beauty pageants, often the winner has narcissistic personality disorder. Miss Congeniality never wins but always has the better personality and family environment. The System knows there is money to be made exacerbating the preoccupation with physical attractiveness.
—Dr. Anthony Napoleon

some recovery tips

Remember to discourage visitors (if you've told anyone) over the first few days. Socializing is a nice idea, but in reality you'll weaken very quickly, no matter how spunky you feel just after your last bowl of soup. The reason for no talking or laughing is to keep everything bound up tight. Extending yourself for company is exactly when you'll pull interior stitches or start some bleeding again. Also, it may be a task to concentrate, let alone respond to a guest. And don't dare jeopardize your new (angular) jawline stretching for tea cakes for

Cousin Louise. You don't need to be remembered in this condition. Besides, to her you'll look beaten and gang raped and she'll be choking back her shock.

my day two

With my straw, I'm surviving on chicken noodle soup from the deli and frozen yogurt (pre-nuked) that I can sip. Most of the pain is retreating, and frankly I feel great. I decide to down another pain pill (on an empty stomach) and attempt to breeze through the *Post*. A few minutes later I drink my soup and cautiously start the walk back to bed.

From my selection of life's lowest moments, vomiting generally equals death. It's always the same. Sickening waves rise from my knees, and heat lightning drenches my scalp. In the same fifteen seconds I feel dizzy and wholly gangrenous, and quarts of saliva rush into my mouth. (I presume somehow I've ingested a squirrel that's been gutter-rotting for weeks.) When my mouth overflows with saliva, I have maybe six seconds left. In my current state of mobility, I'll never make it to the sink. Exploding with sickness I have one thought only . . . *do not pull a stitch* . . . and I don't. Still as a statue, I lean forward from the waist two inches and open my mouth a quarter of an inch. My insensitive soup splashes back out and drips into a Herend bowl. I get instantly clammy and freezing, but I stay braced *in position* in case of a second wave.

I would bargain with God to be pardoned from puking, renegotiable every five years. It was the pain pill on an empty stomach, I'm told. Take them only on top of some minor food, and don't attempt more than three or four steps at a time. If discomfort alone won't restrain you, remember your costly stitches are at stake. After a week, the exterior ones get removed, but the other half you never see. Much deeper, they're still doing their work even after several weeks.

I collapse from the morning's disaster and once again wake up feeling good. My hair is disgustingly greasy, but nothing else is wrong. Being propped up for sleeping feels normal now. No way to inspect my scars with mirrors or torque my head around. I've come upon staples behind my ears, train tracks on top of incisions, running north and due west on both sides. I don't recall hearing about staples, but I wasn't listening well.

They'll be around for a while, it turns out, so make peace with them early on. My routine is to rinse the staples with hydrogen peroxide (use a big dropper; don't pour from the bottle), then apply ointment after they dry. I'm taking Medrol (antiswelling pills), which abruptly stop me from peeing but don't seem to be helping my face.

I resemble a beaten prizefighter who lost the big match last week. Don't be shocked by the discoloration of bruising or glimpses of blood at your suture lines. Though today's not exactly a victory dance, it beats hell out of yesterday. I've known hangovers that were worse.

my day three

I'm having larger energy bursts now between my naps. Not enough to tackle a stack of bills, but enough to feed the cat. The babies finally recognized me today. Maybe just voice and hair color, but in their way they're babbling my name. My first day home, I was the slow-moving stranger in the odd bonnet who collapsed in Mama's room. Finally something about me seems familiar again—more so to them than to me.

Don't be shy about calling your doctor for guidance. Seekers of beauty are often hypochondriachal, and his staff expects to field questions all day. Besides, it's always possible you'll have some development he'll need to know about. You might not get instantly through to your doctor—he'll be in surgery most of the day—but the nurses should give you direction and, at some point your doctor should call. If he doesn't, in my opinion his follow-up care is gravely lacking. I've heard of doctors who never see or speak with the patient again after the surgery's done. You get palmed off to a series of nurses, and finally shown the door. For these guys, everyone *is* just another number.

My dermabraded upper lip could outshine Rudolph's nose. It's bright red and vaguely oozy, so, along with the parts that were peeled, there are burn spots as well. It's a little graphic in general, rinsing incisions and slathering burns, but I feel that I've rounded a corner, and I frankly prefer taking care of my own wounds. If you think it sounds gruesome, *tough it out.* Because all of it works, just not overnight—as long as your doctor is skilled and careful, and you observe the recovery rules. Last night I put a chopped steak with broth in the blender and cherished every drop. Today I decide to nuke a handful of fudge bars and sip the liquid with a baby spoon.

You have to look worse before you look better, and day three was the end of the flu.

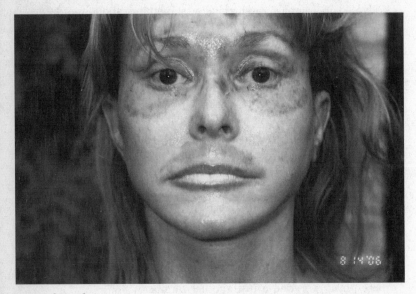

six days after

side view, six days after.

Recovery Reminders
After surgery you must *not*:

- *do any form of exercise for one month*
- *have sexual relations for ten days*
- *lift, bend, or strain (this includes on the toilet)*
- *drive a car for ten days*
- *travel by air for ten days*
- *tweeze, wax, or bleach any facial hair for one month*
- *let your incisions be exposed to direct sun for one month (wear #15 sunblock and a hat on sunny days)*
- *take any aspirin products or vitamin E for two weeks*

any dental work done for four weeks, unless it is an emergency
your weight fluctuate more than five pounds in either direction.

a friend's lift

Several months after my own facelift, a close friend decided to take the leap—partly because I had goaded her, and partly because it was time. I agreed to walk her through it if I could take notes, and she agreed to be my guinea pig. Pig, in fact, is the perfect name for her, since she wouldn't let me use her own.

pig's night before

Pig and I and a mutual friend have an early dinner in a warm, toasty room, though outside it's fairly cold. Pig claims to be "freezing from within" and chilled to the bone. It has to be anxiety, as the rest of us are warm. Pig was having (along with her lift) some dermabrasion on her forehead and a light peel under her eyes. Not many bells and whistles. We make a list of soft things she likes to eat and the people to call when the surgery is done.

Later, she phones from home at midnight (still chilled), to remind me of one last thing. If she somehow becomes a vegetable, she wants all her plugs to be pulled. And in case she dies on the table, I have to agree to cremate her and sprinkle her around Central Park. In fact, over the Sheep's Meadow, since it's her very favorite spot. Five minutes later she phones again with a radical change of plans. Pig had suddenly remembered how herds of rats reputedly cross the Sheep's Meadow at night, and we both know that wouldn't work. So, regarding her unlikely demise, we start again from scratch.

pig in the o.r.

It's exactly four months since my own facelift. Pig's surgery is set for 8 A.M., so she's probably on the table now. It's nicer coming here for a visit than being the plat du jour. Pig will be deep in the groin of the hospital and inaccessible to me. I stand for hours at the entrance to the recovery room and scan it each time the metal doors part to evict another survivor, but there's no sign anywhere of Pig. I phone her doctor's office to see exactly how she did, even though I'm probably fifty feet away from her, through a wall or a hall or two. She's fine, and they cite a room number, suggesting I wait calmly for her there. Her room is cozy and in a corner. Please God, don't let Pig be dying, it's sort of my fault she did this at all.

pig in recovery

Pig breezed her way through surgery but gets stuck in recovery forever. Her gurney exits the elevator, and I get a good look at her face. (The gurney is gliding along swiftly, guided by expert hands.) Her eyes are closed and she's propped up serenely, hands perfectly over her chest. She's wearing a funeral home ssion and hasn't begun to swell. Trotting along beside her I actually *see* the surgical improvements, though they'll soon be obscured for weeks. I am utterly spooked. How could her surgeon know what she looked like fifteen years ago? Because that's who has returned from the O.R. . . . the Pig I knew when she was thirty-five. Eyes still closed, Pig grumbles in a hoarse voice about being thirsty ever since last night's meal. She had been desperate all night for water and can now be fed slivers of ice. Pig quickly gets more lucid and begins to swell before my eyes.

pig's surgery night

Since her lift (8:30 A.M.) she has been blissfully relaxed. She has very little discomfort and doesn't request a pain pill until dinner that night. After her surgery she was written a prescription of Percocet to fill and take home the following day. Snarl number one—the physician's assistant failed to stamp the triplicate form, so it was basically counterfeit. A perfect example of why you should obtain these things in advance. Tomorrow is a Saturday, and if we wait we'll be out of luck. I scramble around her floor and find a doctor to write it again.

Her doctor has urged her not to talk for three days but she is a magpie on the loose. Talking puts strain on the stitches, so I finally leave to discourage her communiqués. I speak with her nurse throughout the night and she does beautifully, almost. Pig talked continuously in her sleep and repeatedly dreamed of having slept through her alarm and missed her surgery entirely.

pig's day one

I arrive at her hospital room early, and she's had a totally comfortable night. Already her doctor has removed her tubes and turban, so I ask if she felt great relief. She hadn't been hurting anyway, so she answers thanks but no. Oddly, Pig was visited by her period in the middle of the night. She did take Medrol for swelling, but compared to me she was barely puffed. After a small lunch of mush, we leave for home and Pig sleeps most of the day. That night she watches parts of a Knicks game and eats soft chicken with applesauce. The last dressing around her head is beginning to chafe, so we phone her doctor (after much deliberation) and he tells us to apply A and D ointment. It works and she is restored.

For weeks, she had feared sleeping through the alarm and missing her surgery date. Pig had no regrets at any moment, though I had quivered through my first day. I slept by her bed on a mattress. She gave me two orders for the night. To bring her fresh ice bags at some point, and a Percocet if she woke up in pain. After the ointment went under her bonnet she slept like an infant till noon the next day.

pig's day two

Shockingly Pig had no actual pain. Discomfort yes, from the swelling, and some itchiness under the bandage, which she was wise enough not to scratch. Pig's eyes have not been surgically touched, but they blow up like little Ping-Pong balls set in the rest of her face. The swelling of her lower lids blocks her downward view to read. She isn't tired so much as impatient, and eager to wash her hair. Her comfort food is cottage cheese with smooth peanut butter mushed in. She is starting to feel like a shut-in and misses daylight, so she takes a small stroll on the terrace with the Ace bandage still on her head. Her dermabrasion wrought zero discomfort unless someone touches it—and yes, then it hurts. What throws Pig into a specially foul mood is being called to the telephone. The receiver can't make contact with her ear at this point, so both listening and speaking aren't great. Finally, Pig activates the speakerphone and she advises that you do too. She continues with only discomfort but takes one pain pill to help her sleep, which again she does very well.

pig's day three

She wakes up merely fourteen hours after she went to sleep. The night before, Pig had groaned about having to lie on her back all night long, preferring to sleep on her side. However, your side is an unlikely refuge, since all cuts converge at your ear. And if one tender zone exists, this is sure to be it. I lent her the pillow I had carved out of foam during my recovery four months before.

pig's pillow

I thought only I had ears sufficiently tender that I couldn't convalesce on my side. I do not have back problems (yet, thank God) but being forever in one position ultimately makes me thrash. I know that sleeping on my face creates facial canyons under normal conditions, so it's gotta be back or sides. My ears are a human fluke. As a country child I could hear a car coming over a mile away—before anyone else had a clue. I took a twerpy delight in announcing this; then within moments, others heard it too. I have no musical talent and have not benefited in any way from my supersonic ears. To the contrary, when everyone else is sleeping, I'm lying there listening to mice converse in the walls.

After the first days of being propped up, I was desperate to flop on my side. But my ears had received the brunt of the lift and it wasn't in the cards. There was, however, one very nice foam pillow my father-in-law had sent us for reading in bed. I located it in the back of a closet and weakly pecked at it with markers, scissors, and duct tape until I had created a nice indentation in the middle for my ear. When it was time to cover it, I thought of all those legendary movie stars who slept only on satin sheets—and who subsequently never suffered wrinkles as badly as the rest of the world. I had remnants of some satin, which I crudely made into the pillow case.

For me it was a miracle. I could rest on my side again. An ear-accommodating, foam pillow that suspended my head straight out from my spine without any contact points near my ear. It saved my life and allowed me to sleep at night, rather than continuing to twitch around in a crooked position, semi-awake. When my ears healed, I stuffed the surgically enhanced reading pillow back into the closet, and frankly hoped it wouldn't be found.

Four months later, Pig's complaints brought the pillow to mind. (For irrational reasons I felt responsible for Pig's lift.) After being so happy with my own, I had determined she needed the same boost, so I goaded, threatened, and coaxed her in that direction. Victory was mine the day I stopped by her building and her doorman announced to her that her daughter was waiting downstairs. (Of course, I'd asked him to say that, but he did it with a straight face.)

I explained to Pig how primitive the pillow was, but she was desperate to give it a try. The morning after, Pig claimed the pillow (suddenly hers) had afforded her an extra five or six hours' sleep. I told her she could keep it, and she sleeps on it to this day. She is now convinced her cheekbone has a niche to rest in, and the satin pillowslip spares wrinkling her face. Though Pig and I remain close friends, I know better than to ask for it back. I have since made at least a dozen more for acquaintances and for doctors with patients recovering from lifts. If my life ever settles down again, I'll market Pig's Pillow somehow in the realm of 800 phone numbers!

my view farther down the road

TWO WEEKS IN:

My body has certainly oozed more than I knew it had to spare. The only discomfort for me is a dull ache behind my ears—like wearing clip-on earrings that look really good but are much too heavy to wear. Or maybe wearing huge tortoise sunglasses that pinch too tightly behind the ears. Again, this seems to be part of my earlobe augmentation, as most people don't have the same complaint. I have to keep remembering it's a process and not a one-day, wand-waving conversion.

THREE WEEKS IN:

The telephone receiver has changed since my surgery. It no longer conforms perfectly to both ears, making the cup it once did. Am washing my hair daily to keep the scars clean. (They tighten up when they dry, so keep them lubricated with your antibacterial ointment.) Only today did I feel flexible and courageous enough to look closely at the area behind my ears.

Recent accomplishments:

- I opened my mouth an inch from tooth to tooth.
- I had a regular meal in a restaurant.
- I abandoned the thin eyebrow brush for brushing my teeth, reembracing my cumbersome toothbrush.
- I have succeeded in not swiveling my body.

- I dazzled my husband with the disappearance of wrinkles he had accidentally referred to as my road map.
- I converted him into a supporter of plastic surgery, at least for women.

FOUR WEEKS IN:

Only tightness around my neck and throat. Could I be coaxed into playing tennis or jogging? Not me. Soon, but not yet—though most facelifted persons are back at their workout regime in two weeks. I'm still wearing camouflage makeup on the peel spots and the areas around my ears, but I no longer need the customized pillow to sleep on my sides, and I'm finally getting fabulous feedback. I'd scheduled a dinner with my control group, which is to say that I had purposely avoided telling one special friend of twenty-five years in order to gauge her reaction. I was terrified. Marie is excruciatingly honest and incapable of telling even a social lie. The moment we sat down she began asking me why I looked so rested—was I taking new vitamins or using illegal facial creams? I could see the questions spinning through her head as she tried to put her finger on what was different. Her eyes frantically searched my face for clues. Had I "done" my eyes, found a new dermatologist? She demanded to know. Only then was I absolutely and completely certain I had done the right thing. For once, this brutally honest woman was flummoxed, confirming my suspicions that my doctor was a genius. His number was instantly shared.

SIX WEEKS IN—PHYSICIAN APPRECIATION PHASE:
Anytime in the six weeks following your facelift, you may be afflicted with Physician Appreciation Phase. Keep your echinacea close at hand and determine to ride it out. Early symptoms are hard to pinpoint, but here are a few I recall:

You may suddenly identify your surgeon as the most sensitive man you know. This can kick in any time after your first two exposures. For example, he comes in as you're recovering to squeeze your hand and find out exactly how you feel. You sense how comfortable he is as a person, especially in this role. His concern feels utterly genuine, unlike a passing cocktail peck-on-the-cheek. Or the "How was your day?" followed instantly by detailed events of his own.

Not so with your surgeon. This human actually cares how you are. He needs to know, in fact. By this time in your life, the purity of such concern so shocks you that you are disarmed. It might force you to recall the last person who inquired about you without pausing to hear your response. For the first time you note what a nice body he has, and it matches his alert concern. You remember how he leaned toward you smiling supportively as you glided toward the O.R. It's not unusual for you as a patient to decide he is the only man you ever met who could truly take care of you. Making your life the way you once thought it could be, probably before you left your parents' home.

You may have known this man for many years but failed to note the inner beauty and utter competence that set him apart

from others. Do not feel guilty because he's married or because you are being unfaithful in your heart. This is your PAP
kicking in. As powerful as any hormone you've ever known,
it's nature's way of fully compensating your doctor. Since
money alone could never do the job, this dripping adulation is
his final payoff.

These moments are delicate ones, comparable to your first kiss.
Be steady and do not get carried away. Remember your pride at
all times. Unless he's a putrid degenerate, he should be savvy
enough and sufficiently gracious to pretend he hasn't a clue. Be
noble and silent in your admiration. Within weeks your perspective will be restored and other men will seem lovely again. It must
be said that the long-term effects of PAP will preserve an inviolate
position for this man in your heart. Though severe, the syndrome
is harmless, a fresh source of gender reinforcement. Long-term
effects are beneficial as well: It may occasionally clarify your perspective on other figures who loom large in your life.

HOW I FELT SIX WEEKS IN:
A viciously truthful and much-therapied friend in her midforties
comes to town for dinner and to see the babies. I had mentioned
my lift weeks before, but distracted by babies underfoot, she had
forgotten. She gasps when she remembers—and immediately
drags me to the brutal overhead lights of my kitchen.

After scrutinizing my face she is floored. She admits I didn't
look pulled or altered, and my wrinkles had seemingly disap-
peared. She briefly even considers I might look younger than her.

All through dinner she is dumbstruck, and I am pretending not to gloat. She is full of life, married to a rock star, and hard as hell to get over a barrel. This alone made the surgery worthwhile.

bobbi's lift

The following is the facelift of Bobbi, who was advised by six doctors not to undergo elective surgery. Bobbi is sixty-two years old and never thought of a facelift until her daughter, who is in retailing, suggested it. She told Bobbi all her clients had lifts and looked great, so her mom should have one too. That started Bobbi thinking, even though her husband was very much opposed. He believes you should live the way you were born and disapproves of cosmetic surgery.

Bobbi's dermatologist gave her the name of two highly recommended surgeons, and Bobbi went for consultations. She has a special problem called "factor eleven deficiency," which can prevent her blood from clotting, but still she felt she could have a successful surgery. In the first consultation, the doctor sat behind an imposing desk and discussed procedures and fees. She felt like "another number," and left. The next consultation was better. The doctor came into the waiting room and spoke with her "as if I were the only patient on earth he would ever have. My internist and hematologist recommended against any elective surgery but I had my heart set on it. Unfortunately, the plastic surgeon agreed [with them]. I was crushed.

"After a year had passed, I went back to the surgeon to see if perhaps I could try laser instead. It was then he told me he had done several cases of factor eleven deficiency successfully, and would be willing to do my lift. I knew, somehow, it would be fine, so I signed a release and scheduled it.

"I checked into the hospital early with no qualms. My plan was to stay for two nights, so my husband wouldn't have to take care of me."

bobbi's surgery day

On Bobbi's surgery day, I communicate only with her private nurse. Her lift and eyes take two and a half hours. Though it is unusual, Bobbi returns from surgery wide awake, with no nausea and no pain. She even wants to talk, but her nurse discourages her. Bobbi has very little swelling or bruising—occasionally she feels uncomfortable from the drains, but likens it to the aggravation you experience from sleeping on curlers. She is given one injection for pain, probably as a preventive, and is given one or two pills for pain during the first twenty-four hours.

She is glad it is over.

bobbi's day one

Bobbi feels "really great" and is out of bed walking down the hall with her nurse at her side. She has no problem urinating, and is accompanied to the bathroom, though it isn't necessary. She is already eating a regular diet (turkey and sweet potatoes for lunch) and her I.V. (purely for hydration) was discontinued that morning. She doesn't want any pain pills whatsoever.

Her helmet dressing is removed along with the drains, and she is still having ice applied. Only at this point has any bruising or swelling begun. She is cheerful and has to be discouraged from talking—including on the phone, which she holds away from her ear. Because her eyes were done, she still has ointment in them and her vision is somewhat blurred. The ointment will be discontinued in two or three days.

bobbi's day two

She claims she has "absolutely no pain." There is temporarily a small tube under her chin, which makes swallowing a little difficult, but the nurse solves that problem with a towel. Bobbi eats all meals (certainly not steak, however), and her husband brings her a milkshake. He has not made one comment about her surgery or the early results. He is five years older than she. Bobbi had a sponge bath earlier and the stitches were removed from her eyes. She has four nurses, each one for twelve hours, putting cold compresses on her. She does not think she is badly swollen or black and blue. Most importantly, a special transfusion stood by her throughout surgery, and she never needed it. Bobbi was not able to store her own blood for the surgery because of her disorder, and she was greatly relieved not to have had a transfusion.

"Even the blood bank can't guarantee it's one hundred percent pure, relative to AIDS."

She goes home at lunchtime. All her nurses are surprised at her minimal swelling. Bobbi just says she "was blessed with good recuperative powers." At home she doesn't have to stay in bed but does rest. She is overwhelmed by how caring the doctor's staff had been. Though six doctors told her no, she had confidence in her surgeon, and rightly so. Her interpretation of all men who disapprove of cosmetic surgery for women is that they find it threatening and intimidating. Her husband still hasn't mentioned her face. "He knows it's my treat to me."

bobbi's days three and four

She still hasn't had one pain pill, except the ones she was given the first night. Her husband picks her up on day two after surgery and drives her home. She fills her prescription for hydrocodone (brand name Vicoden), but sees no reason to take it. When she gets home she continues to apply cold compresses around her eyes and throat while sitting up in her own bed. She rests that afternoon, then her kids come to see her. Her daughter "thinks it's wonderful, my son just shook his head." She later has a nap, eats fish and mashed potatoes for dinner, and goes to sleep at 11:30 P.M. She gets up once in the night to go to the bathroom, then wakes up at 9:30 A.M. She is an amazingly spirited woman.

The morning of day four she is deliberating about whether or not to shower. Her doctor told her to shower, but she feels it might be better to wait a day. She hasn't told any of her friends yet, preferring to be "missing" for three days. She doesn't want them visiting and fussing over her, but she plans to tell them in a week.

five days in:

Bobbi's summation of her facelift is: "I don't look like me yet, but the only place I'm red is around my neck. Aside from that, if I didn't look so terrible I'd go out to dinner. I'm a very active person with a lot of energy. And I do not feel incapacitated in any way."

Dr. Alan Matarasso is her doctor.

the end—and how it began (my own journey)

I returned to my doctor's office for the final inspection a little more than a month after my facelift. Passing the waiting room, I glanced at seven or eight people, both women and men, who appeared most uncomfortably self-conscious. One man was in a business suit, his head hanging down, his right hand covering his face so no one trafficking the halls could identify him. Several women were hunched deep into the upholstery, magazines covering their faces. Not that I was much better—I had arrived in sunglasses and a black fedora that actually comes with detachable hair (thank you Donna Karan). What they felt and I felt made me vividly recall my early teens.

At thirteen years old, the custom in my town was to attend proper dancing school to learn ballroom dancing—clumsy preteens trying to waltz, two-step, and fox-trot. Half the students were girls, half boys. Hour one was all instruction, during which time the boys looked over the girls. The girls were generally miserable, dressed up, wearing trainer bras and our very first stockings (which predated panty hose). This condition alone was traumatic. Hour two was death. We girls were given beribboned dance cards with blank spaces for five names. The cards were tied around each girl's left wrist. At the signal, a clamorous gaggle of boys rushed in all directions to hastily sign up the girls of their choice.

It was over in three or four minutes, after which the other girls appeared to have swallowed canaries. They looked incredibly smug to me. Then, each week our jolly dancing teacher would take me by the hand and trudge to the center of the circular room. She would raise my left hand up with her right, blank card dangling, and repeatedly ask, *"Will someone please dance with Helen Bransford?"*

Silence. The chatter would end and the rustle of motion would cease, as the entire room became embarrassed.

"Will someone *please* dance with Helen Bransford?"

On my best nights, a boy named Pug, not as tall as the rest, would shuffle into the center. Though his eyes were glued to the floor, his stepping forward was a form of consent, and all our stricken faces could quietly relax in relief. I often wish I could find him to thank him for his kindness. Now, thirty-five years and a few stitches later, I'm finally dancing on my own.

As a burning candle
In a holy place
So is the beauty
Of an aged face.

—Joseph Campbell

6

just in case you're

thirtysomething . . .
or even less

good number of procedures that follow in this chapter can be achieved by a fine dermatologist who enjoys focusing on the cosmetic aspects of dermatology. Top dermatologists can perform near-magic with your face (and chest and arms). I think that, had I been in the care of one from my twenties, most of my dilapidation could have been avoided, or certainly postponed. Three giants in this field are Dr. Arnold Klein of Beverly Hills, and Drs. Norman Orentreich and Joel Kassimir of New York City. You might think twice before undertaking a true surgical procedure (such as extensive liposuction, extensive laser, or breast augmentation) with a dermatologist, as they lack the plastic surgeon's anatomical knowledge, though they do have stunning solutions for a broad number of topical problems. If you find a good cosmetic dermatologist (maybe not the one who removes warts and tackles acne), be sure to tell him *everything* about your face that concerns you. Small pockets of fat, a preview of lines between your eyes, red spots or broken blood vessels, a loss of hair, or even an aggressive pimple whose disappearance you would like to accelerate. Exhaust your dermatologist as a resource before moving on to surgery—especially if you're in your thirties. Dermatologists are generally dedicated to postponing surgery and an excellent dermatologist has an enormous bag of tricks. Start working closely with one now, although he *won't* be a substitute for a plastic surgeon. You need them both.

Study this list of procedures carefully. Any one (or two) of these might solve your perceived problem. Some are surgical, some are very simple. Doctors now tend to agree that addressing some of these relatively smaller procedures in your thirties (and sometimes twenties) will leave you with less severe work to do at a later age. Meanwhile, you won't be skidding downhill. And often doing one procedure alone, a combination of several, or a series over several years, can go a long way toward keeping a facelift at bay—though certainly not indefinitely.

1. EYE JOB: IN MEDSPEAK, BLEPHAROPLASTY. A wonderful procedure that removes fat and excess skin from droopy lids and bulging lowers—a giant step toward looking younger and more alert. Often bulging bottoms are inherited and appear prematurely. In other cases, there are repositories of fat and extra skin that have been collecting for years. Popular among males and

females holding competitive jobs in the business community, and those exposed to the public. Excellent bang for the buck.

Back to Work: Ten days after, probably wearing makeup.

Full Recovery: Three weeks to nine months for full results, depending on how you heal.

2. CHEMICAL PEELS. The subject of chemical peels could be a book unto itself. It would cover many different peels in many different strengths. One popular peel, sometimes called a "lunch-time peel," is the glycolic peel applied in a mild solution. Glycolic acid is an alphahydroxy acid (AHA) derived from fruits and other plants. It stimulates new cell growth, which exposes fresher skin. It does not cause permanent lightening of the skin and is a good exfoliating agent for darker skin types. After a light glycolic peel, the patient can reapply makeup and return to normal activities. The new Beta Hydroxy Acid Peel (BHA) stems from salicylic acid and targets primarily acne and very fine wrinkling. Other, less common but very effective peels to inquire about are the Obagi Blue and the Jessner.

TCA Peel (Trichloric acid): A TCA peel can burn away the top layer of withered, wrinkled, or sun-damaged skin. It stimulates new skin growth underneath. It is not an ordeal. Whether sedation is used or not depends on the strength of the TCA, whether or not the TCA is buffered, and the condition of the patient's skin. Hospitalization is not required, and the patient can probably drive home. If you are considering a peel, a good history must be given to your doctor. It should cover whether you have been peeled before, whether you have herpes simplex, whether you are lactating, smoke, use Retin-A, and many other important variables.

Expect swelling, redness, some discomfort, and don't go near the sun. Stick around home the first few days. (Not advisable for African-American, Latino, or Asian skin.)

Back to Work: Varies greatly depending on the strength of the solution and the amount of skin affected. Between three and ten days.

Full Recovery: Ten days.

Phenol Peel: Attacks wrinkles and sun damage on a deeper level, stimulates new skin growth, and bleaches the skin. A far more aggressive approach than TCA. May require one or two days of hospitalization. Skin will be permanently lightened and should no longer be exposed to sun. Expect serious redness and swelling. Longer recovery time than other peels, but also longer-lasting results. Probably far more than you need in your thirties, and much less popular than it has been in the past.

Back to Work: Twenty-one days.

Full Recovery: Three to six months.

3. DERMABRASION. Smooths pockmarks and other scars by giving a consistent contour to the skin. More than a peel, it levels surface irregularities, stimulates new skin growth, attacks wrinkles and sun damage, and eliminates vertical lines leading to your lips. Top layers of skin are mechanically sanded away. When done correctly, the results are miraculous. (Not recommended for African-American, Asian, and Latino skin types.)

Back to Work: If constantly hydrated, maybe one week. Usually closer to two weeks, when makeup is applied.

Full Recovery: May take as much as three months for the redness to fade.

4. LASER RESURFACING. A computer-controlled pulsed carbon dioxide laser is applied to a specific area or to the full face. A dancing ray of light vaporizes one layer of skin at a time, which, when lightly wiped away, instantly reveals for the doctor the condition of the next layer of skin. Anesthesia and a hospital setting are needed. Dr. Gustavo Colon explains that he actually sees one layer of skin vaporize and the layer beneath tighten, like chamois. Sometimes called "laserbrasion," it resurfaces the skin, addresses sun damage and wrinkles, and leaves some tightening of the skin. Healing is more reliable for light-skinned types. Can be applied to the full face or to specific locales, such as under the eyes, smile creases, and the vertically lined area above your upper lip. Relative to peels, there is less swelling and bleeding but a higher incidence of complication and delayed healing.

Laser advocates claim it may prove to have many uses other than skin resurfacing—tooth bleaching and permanent hair removal, for example. Still, much has yet to be learned, and the laser, used improperly, can do significant damage. The Candela laser is able to painlessly zap red spots and broken blood vessels from the face. The ruby laser can remove tattoos as well as brown spots from the hands and arms, and it can resurface wrinkled lips. A new, gentler laser, the Erbium: Yag, is gaining in popularity.

While laser use is becoming more widespread, the key to its success depends upon the proficiency of the doctor, and whether you're a lucky healer (two weeks) or not (five to six months). In unskilled hands, the laser can be harmful. It works best on fair-skinned patients: Patients with olive, brown, or black skin may experience pigmentation irregularities.

Back to Work: For resurfacing, it is dependent on the amount of work done and the individual patient. With makeup, possibly two weeks.

Full Recovery: This varies greatly depending on the extent of treatment and the skin type. Possibly three weeks, possibly five to six months.

5.   BROWLIFT OR FOREHEAD LIFT. Great to move eyebrows back to where they began—on your brow bone. When a drooping brow is lifted, there is usually improvement in the upper eyelids as well. A browlift smoothes furrows in your forehead, and *may* possibly affect your hairline, depending on the type of browlift used. Discuss it with your doctor first. Find out if it will affect your hairline and beware of the Glenn Close look. An endoscopically performed browlift is less invasive, involves less down time, and is generally thought to have shorter-lasting results. This method involves inserting a small tube with a camera in its tip, which shows the doctor on a screen what he's doing. He can watch what he's working on from the inside, and the incisions are smaller. Many doctors, however, are abandoning endoscopic browlifts and returning to hairline incisions. An excellent lift postponer.

Back to Work: Ten to fourteen days with makeup.
Full Recovery: Six weeks plus.

6. FACIAL IMPLANTS. Made of FDA-approved solid silicone, they are placed under the skin, often attached to the underlying bone. Very helpful in correcting an imbalance in the shape of the face. Jaws are squared, cheekbones provide beauty and a bit of lift, and a chin implant can greatly enhance a "chinless wonder." All are subtle improvements that may be hard to identify. When placed correctly, they can cause a very positive reevaluation of a familiar face.

Back to Work: Seven or eight days.
Full Recovery: Four weeks.

7. FACIAL LIPOSUCTION. Applicable even to twentysomethings. Incisions of one quarter of an inch are made and concealed, so fat can be sucked out of the neck or cheek area. Gets rid of baby fat, adult fat, or pockets. Sometimes microsuction is better for small delicate parts (a syringe rather than a cannula). Can give a more craggy look to young men and clean up a fatty chin. The procedure is popular with men, and good for people with good skin elasticity. Recently, External Ultrasonic Liposuction has been used in small areas—such as the face, neck, jowls, ankles, and knees—with good results. Liposuction is *not,* however, a lunchtime procedure, and wearing compression bandages for the treated areas is generally recommended for the first week. Some sedation may be needed.

Back to Work: Five to seven days.

Full Recovery: Two to three months.

Lips are a strong (secondary) sexual cue. All cultures from the beginning of history have modified their lips. In the earliest writings, women painted or pierced them, put plates in them or injured them to make them protrude.

—Dr. Anthony Napoleon

8. LIP ENHANCEMENT. Adds youthful fullness to the lips. Your very own fat may be harvested from another location (like your butt) to protect you from an allergic reaction, then transplanted into your lips. Your own fascia (the tissue that holds your muscles together) can also be used for this in a more surgical procedure, as can the new soft form implant, both of which require anesthesia and are long-lasting solutions, unlike collagen or fat. The soft form implant resembles a spongy tube of spaghetti and can also be threaded into the naso-labial folds (to erase the crease that runs from your nostril to the outer edge of your mouth) or into lips. Some doctors are hesitant to use the soft form, feeling that the margin for surgical error or allergic reaction has not been fully established.

Before you leap, a trial lip enhancement may be achieved by injecting collagen or a temporary filler, showing you what the results would be. The collagen may last only several months but is much more forgiving than the longer-lasting procedures in case you don't like what you see. Thin lips (or "chicken lips") are no longer considered appealing. Think up *one* model who doesn't have lucious lips. Lip enhancement gives a youthful look to men also, though it must be more subtle. Again, before you sign on, try to determine whether you need both lips or only one. It was recommended to me to do only my upper lip.

Back to Work Using Collagen: Same day.

Back to Work Using Fascia or Soft Form: A few days, depending on extent of bruising.

Full Recovery: One week.

9. INJECTABLES FOR THE FACE OR FILLING SUBSTANCES are used to puff out or erase wrinkles, furrows, crow's feet, frown lines, and marionette lines. Most commonly known is collagen (bovine connective tissue that has been boiled down and converted into gelatin). Before racing to have collagen injections, it is important to have *two* sample injections, two weeks apart, to insure that you're not allergic (3 percent are and it's not fun). Collagen lasts four months on average.

The method of injection is most important. Look for a doctor with a true eye for detail, a light hand, and lots of experience. This may call for an excellent dermatologist or a plastic surgeon. Dermatologist Dr. Arnold Klein, for example, has performed over 60,000 collagen procedures. The needle will be placed directly into the wrinkle or tangential to it. With a good doctor, the procedure should be swift, with a minimum of discomfort.

Ask your doctor about other injectables. Dermologen (new on the market) may be the horse to bet on. It's expected to last three times longer than regular collagen, has shown zero allergic reaction, and is derived from human skin cells—easing the minds of those few of us who are queasy about bovine derivatives. Yet another injectable for those who may be having surgery or banking their skin is Autologen, a collagen derived from one's own skin, which also eliminates the concern about allergic reaction. Several injections are necessary, but 75 percent correction is achieved by one year.

Yet another filler, Alloderm, is harvested from human donor grafts and comes in strips that can be cut and contoured to fit exactly the area needed. (Although its uses may be comparable, Alloderm is not an injectable.)

10. BOTOX is a measured amount of botulism toxin that can be injected to paralyze the muscles guilty of leaving horizontal forehead lines, (to a significant extent) crow's feet, and the vertical lines between your eyes that come from squinting or frowning. Some doctors are now skilled at "Botoxing" the neck, which relaxes the look of strained cords. To me, the most astounding aspect of Botox is that once the offending muscle groups are frozen, the wrinkles in that site actually smooth out and disappear. The worst strike against it is its unfortunate-sounding name. If you decide to partake, your doctor will remind you to stay vertical and not exert yourself for four hours, so that the substance doesn't slip and impact the wrong area. Generally effective for six months.

11. BUCCAL FAT PAD REMOVAL. Surgical removal (from inside the mouth) of the cheek's fat pads. The chipmunk look is gone, leaving hollows instead. Though currently popular with young

models, there is a down side. Many doctors warn that as you age and lose cheek fat naturally, you may later look exaggeratedly gaunt. This procedure is appropriate for individuals with "fat cheeks," but usually discouraged for young women trying to achieve a more dramatic look. You can, however, limit the amount of buccal fat that is removed. Though some swelling results, it is countered by the diminished volume of cheek and is usually not noticeable.

12. LATERAL TEMPORAL LIFT, CHEEK LIFT, AND "NEAR LIFT" are partial facelifts that require far less downtime than a facelift and focus on the mid-face, the eyes, or the chin/neck area. Remember to be creative about what you request and focus on your individual problems.

Full Recovery: About two weeks.

So . . .

If you are in your thirties (or even twenties) and feeling a little ragged, do further research on the above and see more than one doctor. A facelift is by no means out of the question, but it is probably more work and more expense than you need at this point.

7

persons

of color

finding the right doctor

i f you are a person of color interested in cosmetic surgery, Dr. W. Earle Matory of Irvine, California, has the following suggestions regarding your choice of doctor.

His suggestions are:

- make sure the doctor is a member of ASPRS and the American Society of Aesthetic Plastic Surgeons (ASAPS)
- ascertain that the surgeon has a working experience of your specific ethnic group and the techniques needed to minimize scarring
- show the surgeon photos of features you like.

Persons of color have, in recent years, shown an increased interest in plastic surgery, possibly due to precedents which have been established by media personalities. Each group has special areas of interest and concern. Be sure the doctor you proceed with has significant working experience with your particular type of pigmentation. Dr. Gustavo Colon urges all prospective patients not to be afraid to ask questions of any doctor; for example, what is his experience, what is his training, and how many times has he performed the procedure(s) in which you are interested on your particular ethnic group.

african-american skin

African-American facial skin has more fibro-elastic support and enhanced support by the bones. The dermis is thicker, has more elasticity, and ages much more slowly than northern European skin, perhaps by twenty to thirty years (according to Dr. Andrew Kornstein). Crow's feet (wrinkles around the eyes) are rarely manifested. Facial fat does not tend to descend, and there is negligible looseness of skin. For these reasons, combined with the extra precaution necessary to avoid scarring, facelifts are not often a favored procedure and are rarely needed. More frequently requested procedures are surgery to elevate the bridge of the nose and thin the nostrils, and chin implants, which are often done together with the nose. Eyelid surgery is popular also, though scarring remains a concern. Buccal fat pad removal is popular because the incisions are made inside the mouth and there can be no visible scarring.

A *keloid* is a raised example of scar tissue resulting from excessive response to trauma or to an incision. Sometimes keloids manifest as a tumorlike outgrowth from a scar. Besides heredity, a keloid can be incited by dirt in a wound, other material imbedded in a wound, or sutures in a scar. If you know you are inclined to develop keloids, surgery is still possible but more complicated. Steroids can be injected into the surgical site at the time the procedure takes place. Generally, after the sutures are removed, the area is injected again with steroids. Later in the healing process, you can use a topical steroid cream. But if even *minor* itching begins, your doctor must be alerted. The smallest amount of rubbing can also incite a keloid to form.

If you are African-American and considering cosmetic surgery, discuss with your surgeon whether an endoscopic approach would minimize your risk of scarring without compromising the results. You are not a perfect candidate for peels, dermabrasion, or laser, as there is a higher rate of pigmentary irregularities.

African-American skin, like all skin, varies greatly in pigmentation. Some is very fair, some very dark. For this reason it would be a mistake to make too many generalizations.

asian skin

It is extremely difficult to make generalizations about Asian or Latino skin because the skin's structure, its texture, and its depth of pigmentation vary greatly from one person to another. The degree of pigmentation is the most important consideration. Among black-haired individuals, the skin type ranges from Mediterranean to the extremely fair; from dark to the equivalent of blond or brunette, and even a very delicate snow-white.

The incidence of keloid scarring is slightly higher than average in Asian skin, though rarer than in African-American skin. Chemical peels and dermabrasion can cause uneven pigmentation, and the laser should be approached very cautiously.

If you are Asian, you probably look ten years younger than your Irish counterpart. One doctor considered his Chinese patient of forty-five to look virtually the same at sixty-five. Facelifts, therefore, are not popular procedures.

Dr. Robert Flowers of Honolulu has a large and distinguished plastic surgery practice, which is equally balanced between Asian and European patients. Generally, Dr. Flowers contends Asian skin is thicker and maintains its quality longer than northern European skin. If a facelift is requested by his northern European patient at forty, it will be requested by his Asian patient at fifty or fifty-five.

Eyes are where you meet the world and meet yourself in the mirror. Eyes are the most important aesthetic unit in the whole body. Healthy, bright, vital eyes give that aura to the whole person.

—Dr. Robert Flowers

Procedures frequently requested by Asians are:

EYELID WORK. The surgery is called "double eyelid surgery" because it places a crease in the upper eyelid, dividing it into two halves. Most eastern Asians have at least small lid folds when they are young, which become obscured with age. (Dr. Flowers strongly advocates raising the brows to restore youthful lid folds). Also known as "Oriental eyelid surgery," double eyelid surgery is less an attempt to look Western than it is to simply deemphasize this feature. Healing time may be longer than standard blepharoplasty and should be discussed in advance with your surgeon.

BREAST AUGMENTATION. This procedure has become very popular among Asian women, who are generally not large-breasted.

NOSE AUGMENTATION. This is popular as it alters scooping bridges and a wide nostril base, heightening the entire nose while also making nostrils more vertical than horizontal.

DERMABRASION. This procedure is performed with caution.

SOME LASER. With pigmentation problems, laser may be contraindicated, though some successful cases are reported. Individual risk factors should be taken up with your doctor.

latino skin

Once again, one's country of origin is less relevant than the degree of pigmentation, or color of the skin. Any abrasion of the skin (dermabrasion, peels or laser) *can* create an imbalance in pigmentation.

sun damage

Sun damage is a reality whether you have light skin or dark, and each person must be aware of his or her own risks regarding sun exposure. Photo-aging and cancer *do not discriminate*. Use a sunscreen of SPF 15 (oil-free if you have oily skin) that contains both UVA and UVB protection. Broad brimmed hats and long sleeves are recommended for *anyone* in the sun, even in seemingly weak winter sun.

8

real men don't get lifts
(they look rested)

The longer I live the more keenly I feel that whatever was good enough for our fathers is not good enough for us.

—Oscar Wilde

*t*he stigma attached to cosmetic surgery has been in retreat since the sixties, which surely marked the dawn of the future cult of youth. The country's oldest president handed over the reins to its youngest ever. At forty-two, John F. Kennedy, Jr., established the twenty-four-karat-gold standard for the meaning of brilliance and youth. He was trim, tanned, and athletic with an even slimmer, more elegant wife. America fell in love with these qualities and the rest of the world followed suit. To be vigorous, outdoorsy, and for the sake of appearances, rich, has been in style ever since.

With an ever-increasing emphasis on youth and fitness, men are rapidly joining the ranks of cosmetic surgery patients. The majority of plastic surgeons are reporting a steady rise in the number of male patients they treat. Dr. Craig Foster's practice in

New York has grown from 10 to 25 percent men in recent years. Dr. Tom Baker of Miami has seen his own quotient of male face-lifts double in the last five or six years. He specifically prefers his male patients to come in by age fifty-five.

The words "God made you the way you are for a reason" used to paralyze us with guilt. Today there is no moral roadblock in the stampede toward self-improvement. Aging football heroes, singers, actors, and weathermen—even televangelists—retain their bright-eyed boyishness from one decade to the next.

My personal theory is that whatever our former First Ladies do (once their husbands are out of office) is okay for everyone else. After the Betty Ford Center was founded, going to rehab became acceptable. And ultimately, even fashionable. Mrs. Ford also squeezed in a facelift, but who would hold that against her? During the early eighties, plastic surgery stepped out of its closet, and the event went totally unremarked. As the nineties come to a close, it's clear that cosmetic surgery is way out of the closet and dancing as fast as it can. Beyond vanity, men now have the excellent excuse of career competition—all those young guys coming up behind them, hungry for bigger jobs—to account for their lifts and tucks. A *Wall Street Journal* study from several years ago revealed the younger and more attractive a man is, the more likely he'll get the job. Unprecedented career competition is, in fact, the strongest factor driving men toward the operating room.

Vanity has no sex.
—Charles Caleb Colton

Consider the sartorially exquisite periods in history we can credit to the vanity of men. Is there any question that King Tut would have cosmetically extended his plumage had plastic surgery been an option? And what about these guys?

Henry VIII of England	*King Leopold of Belgium*
Louis XIV of France	*Louis XVI of France*
Idi Amin of Uganda	*The Marquis de Sade*
Julius Caesar of Rome	*George III of England*
Porfirio Rubirosa	

It's no longer surprising to discover that a man you know has had a lift—maybe that high-profile businessman who, come to think of it, never does seem to age. Guys are catching on in droves, though the numbers do shift geographically: California, New York, Florida, and Texas seem to be leading the way.

> *To love oneself is the beginning of a lifelong romance.*
> —Oscar Wilde

what men want

EYELID WORK. Very subtle, it perks up a man's appearance; a tired, droopy look can become bright and alert. Bags under the eyes can be "refreshed" by going in through the lower lid, thereby leaving no scar.

LIPOSUCTION. The fastest diet of all. "Love handles" and pot bellies are popular targets of this procedure, though everyone has different exercise-resistance pockets.

BREAST REDUCTION. Some men gain weight in the chest that goes to their breasts. Not a cherished look, and easily fixed by a plastic surgeon.

LASER RESURFACING. Attacks wrinkles and sunspots, and may reveal a fresher layer of skin. Can work wonders, depending on whose hand is holding the laser. The surgeon should be experienced with the technique. Full time for healing *may* be as long as three to five months, depending on the individual. Make sure you're a good candidate.

FACELIFT. With a gifted doctor, a weary face, neck, and chin are cleared of extra skin and fat. Done properly, the patient looks well rested and fresh, if not five to fifteen years younger.

For men especially, the result must bring a subtle *improvement. Having dramatic or too-taut surgery is the Universal Fear.*

who are these men?

To start with, anyone who makes his living with his face has surely given it thought. For example, theater, TV, or film actors. Newscasters, spokespersons for companies or products, and models. Potentially any figurehead in any area of life. Even the most enormously successful man has to keep his image in mind. This is likely to include hitting the gym, gulping vitamins, and watching his diet. Being a dish was never easy work.

There's no higher calling than making a
good person look better.
—Dr. Alan Matarasso

Dr. Bruno Ristow advocates lip augmentation for everyone, including men. He feels it is an excellent addition to a man's lift,
and sends subconscious signals of youthfulness without feminiz-
ing. Dr. Harvey Zarem finds men are often happy with the compromise of doing their eyes along with some lipo on the neck and
chin. And Dr. Peter Bela Fodor prefers the near-lift for everyone.
His near-lift includes eyelids, suctioning under the neck, implanting an undetectable chin, and removing buccal fat pads from
the cheeks. Whatever you do, make sure it is work custom-tai-
lored for your own individual face.

A narcissist is someone better looking than you are.
—Gore Vidal

Numerous studies on male facelifts don't exist yet, but I did find
one.* Here's what I learned that might interest you:

• Of the 375 male facelifts evaluated, the average age of the patients was fifty-eight.
• The two largest categories were professionals and business exec-

* "Male Rhytidectomy Revisited," William Stefani, M.D., and Daniel
Baker, M.D.

utives (more specifically, the owners of companies and the top
four executives of companies).

- Any serious complications are likely to occur within ten hours
  of surgery. Generally complications are hematomas—pockets of
  bleeding beneath the skin—and nerve damage, which is both
  rare and nearly always temporary.
- Patients who experienced complications also had much higher
  than average diastolic blood pressure.
- Success in lowering the rate of complications was attributed to
  aggressively monitoring both blood pressure and any small incidence of bleeding that occurred.
- Camouflaging incisions is more complex than in women. The
  patient's beard, hairstyle, and sideburns have to be carefully
  assessed. The skin from the top of the neck/jaw area has to be
  pulled up, and the patient may now have to shave the area
  behind his ears.

The seeming conclusions are that preexisting conditions, such as
high blood pressure, diabetes, or vascular problems are indicators
of possible post-surgical complications.

Men, more than women, seem to be self-conscious about being
seen in a plastic surgeon's waiting room. If you feel this way,
prearrange on the phone to arrive through a separate entrance or
be guaranteed as much privacy as possible.

In advance of your surgery date, establish a foolproof support
system to help you through recovery. This includes a
predesignated person (a private nurse rather than your lover) to

help you round the clock for at least the first thirty-six hours. You could use some help for longer than that, but the first thirty-six hours are critical. The whole healing process takes men slightly longer because, for one thing, their skin is thicker than a woman's.

Whether you are a businessman or an artist, you won't be running the show for a couple of days after your facelift. Activate the plan you would use for running your office in absentia, just as you might for a trip overseas. You're not likely to be the exception to the rule that you usually are, nor will you be bungee-jumping next weekend. You may have to relearn to shave. And be sure to remember to have soft foods for meals, and nothing that's highly spiced. If you're watching your weight, this is a good time for liquid meals, as long as they're reasonably balanced. Have someone keep things tidy, and above all, get a lot of rest. Hang up your Boss hat and slip into a gown.

tips specifically for men:

- Because of your manly stubble, your blood pressure has to be carefully monitored. Each hair follicle in your beard has its own blood supply, which leads to more bleeding than is generally seen in women. Some doctors may ask you not to shave prior to surgery and to resume shaving one week after, but with an electric shaver.
- A man's skin is thicker and more oily than a woman's—and

guess who ages better? With the hide a little tougher, it's slightly more strenuous for the doctor, though certainly a manageable task.

- In order to look natural, a strip of skin must be left in front of your ear, to separate it from your sideburn. Discuss this with your doctor. He will have to take extra care hiding your scars, since presumably your hair is fairly short. If you can pull it off, consider growing a beard for six months and shaving right before surgery. People will then be more confused about what has actually changed.

- When giving your history, do not gloss over your real-life vices or any aspect of your health with any member of your medical team.

- Don't be afraid of being sedated. Relax and go with the flow.

- Alert your doctor if, after the surgery, you experience sharp, throbbing pain that doesn't respond to medication, or a marked increase in swelling in a particular spot.

- Don't race back to anything that might raise your blood pressure or pop an interior stitch. (Sex is exactly what I mean.) Check with your doctor about when and how you might resume your normal habits—even the supposedly unstrenuous ones.

it's not easy being a guy . . .

It's constitutionally harder for a man to ask for help, but in this instance it's imperative. You should try to consider yourself an invalid. You won't be, but that attitude would be helpful.

According to Dr. Robert Goldwyn at Harvard,* the average man

- has a lower threshold for pain
- is less able to handle stress
- has a less stable cardiovascular system
- is more inclined toward cardiovascular disease
- requires substantially more anesthesia
- has less tolerance for lying still

and if I may add,

- is less willing to follow instructions
- and more embarrassed by physical compromise.

* *The Patient and the Plastic Surgeon*, Dr. Robert Goldwyn (Little Brown, 1991), p. 143.

one man's lift

"I'm the perfect candidate. I've always been jowly and I've lost seventy-five pounds. It made my skin really sag. That, combined with age, made me do it. It's as simple as pie.

"I chose Jack Fisher, who previously was on the staff at Mayo, and I wasn't nervous. On my second visit I took Jack a photo of me in my last year of college—and darned if I didn't come out looking just like that but with a little less hair.

"I went in for surgery on Wednesday. Sunday was going to be Christmas. I told my wife and she didn't like it. My kids laughed at me. I'm an enormously energetic person. So on Wednesday I did a little desk work then went to the Institute (the Baptist Hospital Institute for Aesthetic and Reconstructive Surgery, Nashville). I waited in a holding room while they drew all over my face. After that they wheeled me into surgery. It might have taken longer than usual because with my weight loss, I had excess skin.

"When I woke up I remember talking to my doctor and my wife. I had no pain. None whatsoever. In fact, I never had any pain. Then I pretty much slept until the following day. My doctor says part of it is recovering from the anesthesia. By the way, I'm fifty-three.

"On the second day after surgery . . . well you're not supposed to do this, but I drove myself home. I rested, but I wasn't hurting. That night I went to a neighborhood party with my bandage still on. They were all pretty close friends.

"Saturday was Christmas Eve, and we went to a big family

dinner. The next day was Christmas and we entertained all day. I rested on Monday, and Tuesday I was back at work. He did a lot of work on my face, but he didn't do my brow, for one reason I'm partly bald. The following weekend I was in black tie and dancing.

"I think attitude has a lot to do with it. I'm a self-assured person. I didn't do it for competitive reasons relating to business. It was more that after I lost the weight I took pride in my appearance.

"Everybody says your eyes will be terribly swollen. I had no bruising, and my eyes had always been puffy, so that was nothing new. They do move your beard around a little bit. I had to learn to shave all over again. But I felt completely well in one day's time. Thirty to thirty-five percent of the patients in the Institute are men now."

After all, where do you draw a line in the gray area between using Minoxidil and having a lift?

These famous faces are said *to have had some work:*

Merv Griffin	Sylvester Stallone	Chevy Chase
Johnny Carson	Jack Lemmon	Robert Towne
George Hamilton	Kirk Douglas	David Bowie
Siegfried and Roy	Cliff Robertson	Richard Dreyfuss
Peter Gabriel	William Shatner	Tony Bennett
Joe Namath	Robert Stack	Elvis (in a Las
Dick Clark	Dame Edna	Vegas hotel room
David Mahoney	Pete Townsend	converted for the
George Jones	Joel Grey	occasion)

These guys have actually taken the blows and prevailed without a lift. It hasn't cost them a thing. I like to think of their abstinence as the last vestige of chivalry on earth.

Sean Connery	*Mick Jagger*
Robert Mitchum	*Joel Schumacher*
Clint Eastwood	*Montel Williams*
Robert Redford	*Jeff Bridges*
Colin Powell	*Muhammad Ali*
Harrison Ford	*Denzel Washington*
Jimmy Buffett	*Mel Gibson*

Finally, what I want to say is, what's good for the goose is now dandy for the gander.

9

the cosmetic
future

*Be not the first by whom the new are tried, nor yet the last
to lay the old aside.*

—Alexander Pope

*t*he future of plastic surgery is unquantifiable. The current
array of available procedures would have been unfathomable to our grandparents. Or to Betsy Ross. I'm starting to
believe in the Christian Scientists' "Whatever the mind can con-
ceive, man can achieve."

I know that cellulite is high on the list of targets for the future.
And that laser will boast some diverse new claims: laser for depil-
atory use, laser for cleaning your teeth, laser work on the lower
eyes (using the laser as a cutting tool and to smooth the contour
as well), and laser application to body parts for reshaping and
shrinking. Endoscopic facelifts may have a place among highly
selective patients. And autologous fat grafting sounds both excellent and long-lasting as an answer to deep creases, depressions, or
facial atrophy—the secret to its success lies in a new and deeper

method of inserting the fat. Surgeons in the future may be wearing virtual reality visors for some procedures, which will prevent them from having to turn from the surgical site to coordinate with a computer screen. And it is posited that breast implants made of soybean oil and encased in silicone shells might contain a microchip to report on the condition of the implant.

Ultrasonic assisted liposuction (UAL) is bound to mushroom across the country in the near future. Having originated in Italy, the technology is being refined by a team of brilliant U.S. doctors working closely with the FDA. A tiny cannula is inserted through a small incision and liquefies any fat it encounters, then evacuates it in its melted form. UAL's advantage to a patient over standard liposuction is significantly less blood loss, less trauma to the body, and reportedly no damage to the connective tissues, which encourage the skin to shrink as an adjunct of healing. I expect UAL, as it is technically perfected, will be added to many doctors' repertoires and will be extremely popular as a procedure. So far, its highly experienced pioneer in the United States is Dr. Pat Maxwell of Nashville, and top among his students in learning the technique is his colleague, Dr. Mary Gingrass.

dr. 2000

Here is a profile of John Korzelius, the most radical doctor I met in my travels. He may be a genius of aesthetics or a madman creating an Olympic beauty team. Although he completed his medical education brilliantly, he had no desire to become board certified as a plastic surgeon. He's no darling of the medical community and belongs to no organizations, making it difficult to accumulate information on him. He could be the ultimate aesthetician (a possible precurser of doctors to come) or an unruly pirate of his profession. The conservative standards observed by most plastic surgeons hold no interest for Dr. John.

His patient population seems to include a hefty chunk of the Already-Beautiful, and of the Well-Established Young. He informed me that any twenty-four-year-old model making $100,000 a year will already have had some "work" (maybe breasts, lipo, or a lateral lift to give her eyes an exotic look). Furthermore, there are only five top cover girls, and by the age of thirty-two *all* of them have had something done (ever notice how they disappear for a bit and return with a hairdo that's new?).

Korzelius refers to these women namelessly with what may be fatherly pride, and he complains (quite sincerely) about the lack of decent acting parts for leading ladies over thirty-five. I asked him about trends for the future and he was candid: "Lips are huge [long-term lip augmentation, that is], and lateral lifts are increasingly sought."

One rumor circling the Valley is that Michelle Pfeiffer consulted him while she was still very young. She's a pro I respect and cheer for, and a rumor doesn't detract from her talent. She was inarguably pretty to start with (just revisit *Into the Night*). Then, I am told, she consulted Dr. John, who supposedly envisioned what she *could* be. He made her nice eyes mesmerizingly exotic and augmented her already original lips. She is now an unforgettable beauty—but perhaps that's just how she matured. Dozens of famous—and often young—women are rumored to be handing their reins over to him. It's not hard to unearth the list of names, but for their sake, I'll stop here. If any of the rumors are true, Ms. Pfeiffer is in good company.

Korzelius sees surgery as an athletic event, demanding excellent technical judgment and creativity at the same time. He claims to be present in New York when the U.N. meets, for prearranged consultations. And he has operated on one or two international figureheads whose security teams required him to cross oceans to perform. For the last decade he's turned out 1,200 major surgeries as well as 150 facelifts every year. And he swears to a complication rate of less than 1 percent.

The vast majority of human beings dislike and even actually dread all notions with which they are not familiar. Hence innovators have generally been persecuted, and always derided as fools and madmen.

—Aldous Huxley

some politically incorrect thoughts from dr. korzelius:

- He considers Los Angeles's plastic surgery eight or ten years ahead of New York's and fifteen years ahead of the rest of the country.
- He sees the East Coast medical community offering less opportunity for creativity and progress. He claims that what counts in the Northeast are your pedigree, where you went to school, and

your intellectual credentials. In L.A. it's simply how you look and what you've accomplished. Physical appearance rates higher there.

• He's concerned that the established medical societies view change as being not good.

• He feels plastic surgery programs offer better training for microsurgery and reconstructive than they do for cosmetic work. In the academic world, he claims, cosmetic surgery lacks the prestige of reattaching a limb (which would be plastic surgery, but reconstructive rather than cosmetic).

• As he reads it, surgeons working the front lines and making the changes aren't the guys in the establishment's "little" clubs.

Korzelius's academic credentials seem golden (I reached one plastic surgeon who trained him at UCLA, and who gave him unqualified praise for brilliance. He was disappointed to learn Korzelius never took the boards and claims he no doubt would have aced them. Yet another top-notch surgeon in Beverly Hills calls Dr. John the P.R. nightmare of their field.

Scads of mothers bring Korzelius their fourteen-year-old daughters to be evaluated. Each hopes her daughter has the makings of a supermodel, if Korzelius can spot what she needs to have fixed. Meanwhile, many patients of Dr. John have cleverly gotten facelifts before their mothers have even given it a thought.

Korzelius is unusual, unorthodox, unpretentious, and charming. But board certified he is not.

products of the future

Dr. Joel Kassimir, who succeeded early on with excellent micro-transplants for the hair (now the most successful procedure) will be unleashing a new product: a topical cream that somehow, over a month's time, appears to shrink the herniated fat beneath the eyes by 50 percent or more. Imagine Mario Cuomo after a few months with Dr. Kassimir's cream! (It's due out this year under the name "Ageless Eyes.")

For those of us who overindulged in sun, there are numerous remedies on the horizon. One doctor I know has developed a cream, applicable to the chest and arms, which attacks pre-cancerous spots, essentially reversing sun damage. Ever see a beautifully restored face with elephant skin on the chest, arms, and hands? A dead giveaway.

Meanwhile, a New England company has perfected the storage of those extraneous skin bits that are normally discarded in surgery. From this banked skin, your own collagen can be easily extracted, thereby eliminating the possibility of an allergic reaction. This collagen (Autologen) is stored at minus eighty degrees and can be used for years to plump out wrinkles. But beyond any cosmetic use, it can be used in the neck of the bladder to end incontinence following prostate surgery, and for the thousands of elderly who experience incontinence as well. (Many estimate that more diapers are sold for the elderly than for infants.) Finally, for victims of cancer of the larynx, Autologen can be used in the vocal chords to restore speech. Some doctors now remind patients to consider banking skin from routine surgeries to address a range of future problems.

Some surgeons are battling the aging process from within. Dr. Norman Orentreich, the distinguished New York dermatologist, has conducted groundbreaking research in the area of antidisease and antiaging hormones over a period of forty years. A pioneer in the field, he published the first paper establishing that the production of DHEA decreases with age, and more than twenty years ago he was making up cream formulations for his patients that incorporated DHEA and progesterone. Today, at age seventy-four, Dr. Orentreich vigorously continues his work and research, and is routinely mistaken for a man in his fifties.

Others active in the field are Dr. Steven Hoefflin and Dr. Mark L. Saginor, whose Anti-Ageing Institute in Santa Monica focuses its research on the decrease in our hormones as we age. The Institute addresses safely revitalizing the body through the use of such hormones as DHEA, growth hormone, estrogen, progesterone, and testosterone. It also offers alternative approaches to medicine, which include various herbs, vitamins, minerals, micronutrients, and medications. Its goal is to protect against age-related problems such as memory loss, heart disease, osteoporosis, general muscular weakness, and cancer. The results to date are dazzling.

Personally I'm waiting for an ultrasonic beam to cleanse and condition my hair without getting it wet.

As far as I can see, anything is possible.

*Every great advance in science has issued from a new
audacity of imagination.*
                                                    —John Dewey

*Any new instrument is only an extension of the surgeon's hand,
reflecting his knowledge and experience over youth.*
                                                    —Dr. Frank Kamer

Appendix

The doctors quoted or referred to in this book:

Dr. Sherrell Aston, New York City
Dr. Daniel Baker, New York City
Dr. James Baker, Winter Park, Fla.
Dr. Thomas Baker, Miami
Dr. Jay Burns, Dallas
Dr. James Carraway, Norfolk, Va.
Dr. Gustavo Colon, Metairie, La.
Dr. Bruce Connell, Santa Ana, Calif.
Dr. Jack Fisher, Nashville, Tenn.
Dr. Robert Flowers, Honolulu, Hawaii
Dr. Peter Bela Fodor, Los Angeles
Dr. Craig Foster, New York City
Dr. Simon Fredericks, Houston
Dr. Jack Friedland, Phoenix
Dr. Mary Gingrass, Nashville, Tenn.
Dr. Robert Goldwyn, Brookline, Mass.
Dr. Mark Gorney, Napa, Calif.
Dr. Ronald Gruber, Oakland, Calif.
Dr. Roxanne Guy, Melbourne, Fla.
Dr. Sam Hamra, Dallas
Dr. Vivien Hernandez, Boca Raton, Fla.
Dr. Steven Hoefflin, Santa Monica, Calif.
Dr. Debra Johnson, Sacramento, Calif.
Dr. Frank Kamer, Beverly Hills
Dr. Joel Kassimir, New York City
Dr. Stanley Klatsky, Baltimore
Dr. Arnold Klein, Beverly Hills
Dr. Andrew Kornstein, New York City
Dr. John Korzelius, Burbank, Calif.
Dr. Malcolm Lesavoy, Beverly Hills

Dr. Alan Matarasso, New York City
Dr. W. Earle Matory, Irvine, Calif.
Dr. G. Patrick Maxwell, Nashville, Tenn.
Dr. Peter McKinney, Chicago
Dr. Foad Nahai, Atlanta
Dr. Anthony Napoleon, San Diego
Dr. Norman Orentreich, New York City
Dr. Ivo Pitanguy, Rio de Janeiro, Brazil
Dr. Thomas Rees, Santa Fe, N. Mex.
Dr. Bruno Ristow, San Francisco
Dr. Blair O. Rogers, New York City
Dr. Mark Saginor, Santa Monica, Calif.
Dr. Robert Schermer, Los Angeles
Dr. Susan Craig Scott, New York City
Dr. George Semel, Beverly Hills
Dr. Frank Thorne, Seattle, Wash.
Dr. William Wennen, Fairbanks, Alaska
Dr. Harvey Zarem, Beverly Hills